The Pleasure of His Company

LIFE-
CHANGING
ENCOUNTERS
WITH
JESUS

LEE VENDEN

REVIEW AND HERALD® PUBLISHING ASSOCIATION
HAGERSTOWN, MD 21740

The author assumes full responsibility for the accuracy of all facts and quotations as cited in this book.

This book was
Edited by Richard W. Coffen
Designed by Patricia S. Wegh
Illustrations by Darrel Tank
Typeset: 12/14 Berkley Book

PRINTED IN U.S.A.

99 98 97 96 95   10 9 8 7 6 5 4 3

R&H Cataloging Service
Venden, Lee
     The pleasure of His company: life-changing encounters with Jesus.

     1. Jesus Christ—Stories.   I. Title.
          232.904

ISBN 0-8280-0825-6

Dedication

This book is dedicated to Marji, for continuing to hold the vision before me; Morris, for showing me how to spend the "thoughtful hour"; Marilyn, for teaching me to pray; Clare, for his persistence in encouraging this project; Barbara, who clung to His hand through the valley of the shadow; and Ellen, for her inspirational words.

Acknowledgment

I am indebted to a student of mine, Elvira Jim, for her own sanctified imaginings, which provided the basis for "Where Are Your Accusers?"

Contents

Tell Me Again

Introduction

Many years ago, while reading *The Desire of Ages*, I came across this statement: "It would be well for us to spend a thoughtful hour each day in contemplation of the life of Christ. We should take it point by point, and let the imagination grasp each scene, especially the closing ones. As we thus dwell upon His great sacrifice for us, our confidence in Him will be more constant, our love will be quickened, and we shall be more deeply imbued with His spirit" (p. 83).

Since that time I have gathered and read as many books on Jesus' life as I could find. I have read and reread about His life in Scripture and have often pondered the closing verse of John's Gospel: "And there are also many other things which Jesus did, the which, if they should be written every one, I suppose that even the world itself could not contain the books that should be written" (John 21:25).

I have prayerfully tried to imagine what some of those "things that Jesus did" could have been. I have studied inspired writings, looking for minor details that could help fill in some of the gaps in the greatest story ever told. I have tried to use imagination to put myself into the story as an observer. And I *have* found my love for Him "quickened."

This book would be best used as a tool to spark your own sanctified imaginings. If the old, old story takes on new life and if your appreciation for Jesus grows, then He is to be thanked.

SonLight

(BASED ON JOHN 1:1-18)

WHEN IT ALL BEGAN, HE WAS NOT ALONE.
WITH HIS FATHER HE LIVED IN A WONDROUS HOME.
ALL THINGS WE TASTE, HEAR, FEEL, AND SEE
CAME FORTH THROUGH HIM FROM ETERNITY.

IN HIM WAS LIFE, AND THE LIFE WAS LIGHT.
IN HIM WAS GLORY, POWER, AND MIGHT.
AND THE LIGHT SHINES ON, THOUGH DARK CAN'T KNOW,
THOUGH MANY REJECT WHAT HE CAME TO SHOW.

THE LIGHT SHINES ON AND *SOME* DISCERN.
ONLY THOSE REBORN EVER START TO LEARN.
BUT ALL WHO *SAW* HIS FLESH AND FACE
RECEIVED OF HIS FULLNESS, GRACE FOR GRACE.

AND ONE WHO WROTE ABOUT THIS MAN
(WHO WAS WITH HIM WHEN THE FLESH BEGAN
TO TEACH AND HEAL AND WALK OUR SOD)
CALLED THE LIGHT THE SON OF GOD.

ACROSS THE YEARS THE LIGHT SHINES STILL.
HE'S SHOWN HIMSELF; AGAIN HE WILL.
FOR THOSE WHO LOOK, HE'S THERE TO SEE!
. . . *THE PLEASURE OF HIS COMPANY.*

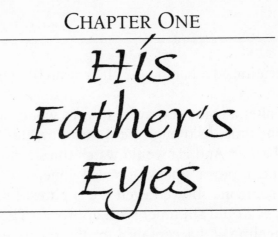

CHAPTER ONE

His Father's Eyes

He had His mother's smile and dimpled cheeks. He had her auburn hair, her nose, her mouth. He had the music of her voice and laughter . . . but He had His Father's eyes.

As wind sweeps across the surface of a lake, changing its shadows, ripples, reflections, and colors, so life swept across His eyes. And those who looked into them knew that they were looking through the windows of His heart and soul.

His eyes contained the freshness and purity of a snow-fed mountain stream. They were a place where winter was melting into music. In them was the energy, the vitality, and the enthusiasm of One who loved people. A deep-breathed zest for living!

Often as He gazed skyward, His eyes, like crystal pools, would seem to reflect heaven. And sometimes at sunset they were ablaze with red and golden fire—more a part of heaven than of earth.

Other times they would sparkle like the sea as He sailed with friends across the shimmering waters of Lake Galilee. There would be wind in His hair and a tingling of spray upon His cheek.

When He was a child, the wide-eyed innocence of youth mingled with pain as He saw and understood the significance of the sacrificial service.

When He worked in the carpenter's shop, His eyes were the eyes of a craftsman as he scrutinized a handmade chair, searching meticulously for defects or errors.

Sometimes after a night in prayer His eyes would seem to hold the memory of a bygone time. As though He were a time traveler to whom the present posed no barrier. And He would watch the sunrise as one who looks with satisfaction and approval upon a job well done.

Whenever someone showed even the slightest kindness to a brute or fellowman, His eyes would shimmer with approval. They were full of patience for the struggling and acceptance for the repentant—no matter the sin. Looking for the lonely and offering a smile, they would sweep across a crowd. Always they contained compassion for the friendless, the losers, the outcasts. And they had empathy for those not blessed with the looks or the charm that makes one popular with the superficial crowd. Understanding.

They would twinkle good-naturedly when children pulled on His beard or robe. And His eyes were laughter as He tumbled with youngsters down the grassy slopes of springtime, or played tag with them, or skipped stones across the rippled surface of Galilee.

There was humor of another sort in those eyes as He answered a pharisaical question with another question or began an exposé by saying, "Consider another parable . . ." The tale would conclude with a look that penetrated deceit and hypocrisy, and that read the most secret thoughts.

Though filled with tears, His eyes at times were nonetheless stern— even fierce—as He flexed a powerful forearm while sweeping out His Father's house. One could see pain that was difficult for Him to disguise as He witnessed evil or injustice.

One time they brought a woman to Him, and His eyes brimmed over at their thoughtlessness and her shame. As He said to her, "Daughter, neither do I condemn you," His eyes revealed the same love and care that was present when He'd return a fledgling to its nest.

Gentle were His eyes as He stroked a fevered brow, and sympathy as He listened to a father pleading for the life of his child.

As He spoke to the crowds, one could see in His eyes an anxiousness, a hoping. There was longing in them as He searched for response from the hearts of calloused and indifferent people. There was wonder that they could listen and not hear, look but not see, come but not allow more than their bodies to be healed. And sorrow would linger as men and women sought Him for food or health and then left upon receiving it.

At times a spark of happy recognition could be seen as He noticed someone in the crowd who had been there before, listening and smiling. But there was sadness also, for most left with their loaves and fishes. Sadness as the disciples slept instead of praying. Sadness as He continued walking and working alone, despite the crowds that gathered. Always alone.

Concern shone in His eyes that many would never respond, never realize who was passing by. Even Philip said, "Show us the Father and it will suffice," and those who heard the reply "Oh, Philip, have I been with you so long and still you say, 'Show us the Father'?" also noted in His eyes a shadow of despair.

One could see, however, a renewal of courage and the return of a sparkle as He came forth morning by morning from talking with His Father. Early predawn winds would blow their own energies into Him, and cares would drop away like the leaves of autumn. In His eyes would be joy! Joy also as Peter proclaimed, "You are the Christ, the Son of the living God!" Joy as Greeks from the West said, "We would see Jesus!" Joy as a dying thief called Him Lord!

Just now there is longing and wistfulness in His eyes as He walks through the empty streets and mansions of His Father's house. Desperately He wants to say, "Welcome home, children!" Eagerly He's waiting to hear laughter in those streets. Anxiously He's waiting to be reunited with His friends. Oh, His eyes are going to fill with joy turned to glory when He can finally say "Lo, I come!"

He told us that if we had seen Him, we had seen the Father. He had His Father's eyes. And all who saw them felt, though they stood upon the earth, that they were gazing into the very eyes of God.

CHAPTER TWO

Eye Witnessed

Standing in the Jordan River, I watched the azure dome crack and glory come streaming through. At first I was so blinded that I turned away, but a voice bade me look again, and as I did I felt a strange burning sensation, as though a cover or lens had fallen from my eyes. In that same instant I was aware that distance no longer affected the clarity of my vision.

I looked through a corridor in the heavens that appeared to be lined on either side by planets, stars, and galaxies. Light flowed like a river down the passageway. Light so pure, so complete, that it seemed to have substance and form. It was clear and yet opaque—radiant, shining, rising, falling, expanding, moving like vapor on a winter's morn.

As I looked farther along this luminescent pathway through the stars, I saw with wonder the Source from whence it flows. Strangely, the farther I gazed, the clearer I saw. There, in brilliant detail, at the end of the corridor (or was it the beginning?) was a city.

Its walls were made of light—luminous as burnished gold in the sun. Its foundations were 12 colors of the rainbow, so rich, so pure, so brilliant, that I wondered whether they might be the source or fountainhead of color. But my eyes were drawn upward, above this city of light and color, and there, blazing in glory beyond description, was a throne.

He who sat upon it shone with the unborrowed magnificence of 10,000 suns. The glory that came from Him was divided into colors, as a prism separates light; but unlike a prism's colors, these were not refracted. They began with Him. Colors, as smoke, mingled and blended about the throne. Letters of fire were engraved upon it, blazing the words: HOLINESS, JUSTICE, TRUTH, LOVE, PURITY, ALPHA, OMEGA.

And the river of light streaming down the corridor burst into music, as the voice of many waters, singing, "Glory, glory, glory!" And I saw and knew that the river, and the stars, and the universe, and the earth, and all things bright or beautiful had their source in Him! I dropped to my knees and worshiped.

Then, from amongst the light about the throne, I saw the form of a Dove take shape. Its wings were like the city—luminous as burnished gold. Its eyes were flames so pure, so bright, that the path of light dimmed before their brilliance. It circled the throne three times, and then with a rushing of wings and scattering of light, it flew swiftly toward me. The music of the river struck a note higher as the Dove's wings fanned the air above it.

As it drew closer, another thing happened. Light began shining from the face of the Man before me. Like the glory round the throne, that which shone from Him was not reflected. He was the source. And the light streaming from His eyes was by far more brilliant than the sun. While He stood gazing upward, the Dove lit in dazzling splendor upon His head.

And a voice was heard, like the sound of many waters. The heavens trembled and the earth shook. The sound seemed to come from everywhere yet nowhere. It echoed and rumbled across creation, and the words spoken were these: *"This is My beloved Son in whom I am well pleased!"*

Then suddenly, as though heaven and earth had inhaled . . . all was still. In the same instant it was dark. I thought my eyes had failed me, but as I grew accustomed to the darkness, I saw dim shapes of people here and there.

I looked up once again and saw, flickering dimly like a candle in a cavern, the sun. I wondered how it had grown so feeble, and I realized then that it had not been changed except by the glory my eyes had seen.

I turned my gaze earthward, searching for the One I had just baptized. He was kneeling upon the riverbank, where a subdued but holy light still shone about Him—silent reminder of the glory that had been.

I looked around at the people gathered about and read the expressions on their faces. Only a few seemed entranced, but all were gazing at Him, though many seemed full of idle curiosity. Others appeared puzzled or looked confused. All were silent—wondering.

But I saw, and now bear record, that this was the Son of God!

CHAPTER THREE

Where Are Your Accusers?

The wind caressed His face and played with His hair. His upturned face glowed with the light of the star-studded sky. The cold bit through His robe, and His body ached with the strain of the day before. With distress of mind, He stood alone, thinking. Usually He was able to shake this loneliness that sometimes engulfed Him, but tonight was different. Tonight it seemed as though it just might conquer Him.

Doubt filled His mind with questions about His effectiveness on earth. It was hard to understand why the people could not grasp the reason for His teaching or His deep concern for their welfare. At times it seemed hopeless, but because He loved them, He knew He could not give up.

From where He stood He could see the sleeping city below. The empty streets and shops would soon be filled with people. He longed to teach them what His Father was *really* like, but His time was short and their hearts seemed dulled to understanding.

He sat down on a rock and put His face in His hands. His mind drifted back over the past. Back through the struggle in the wilderness and His baptism, all the way to His childhood. All this He remembered as though it had happened yesterday. But one event stood out. It had occurred when He was just a boy . . .

The weather had been beautiful that day long ago. He had finished breakfast and gone to draw water from the well for His mother. Though not quite 11, He was big for His age, and the work He did for His father in the carpentry shop had greatly strengthened Him.

He was not far from the well when He came upon a small group of boys teasing a young girl. The girl came from a home that was ostracized because her father was a tax collector for the Romans. He had heard her being teased about it before.

She must have come for water also, because her jar lay broken a short distance away from where she stood. The boys surrounded her to prevent her escape, taunting her mercilessly.

"Your daddy's a Roman!" shouted one.

"Traitor!" screamed another.

Then one of them grabbed her shawl. She cried out, trying in vain to get it back. They tossed it back and forth among themselves, letting it fall in the dirt. Suddenly, while chasing one of them, she tripped on her skirt and fell to the ground. The boys laughed and jeered as tears welled up in her eyes and streaked her face.

He quickly set His jar down and began running to her rescue. He had almost reached her when an adult voice rang out.

"Jonathan, get back over here this instant! Hurry up with that water!" A heavyset woman was walking down the path. Red-faced and winded, she grabbed one of the boys by the ear and dragged him after her. The rest of the group scattered to avoid similar punishment at the hands of their mothers.

He went over to where the girl's shawl was and picked it up. He brushed off the weeds, then walked over to her and held out His hand to help her up. Her black hair was matted, and she looked up at Him through muddy brown eyes, as though expecting Him to laugh or throw the shawl in her face. All she saw in His eyes, however, was compassion.

She took His hand, and He pulled her up and handed her the shawl. "Thank You," she whispered as she turned away from Him and started home.

"Wait!" He called. "Here, take My jar. But let Me fill it with water for you first." He turned to the well and swiftly drew up the water. After He placed the jar in her arms, He helped arrange the shawl about her shoulders. He watched her turn and make her way back up the path to her home before returning to His own. His parents had understood about the missing jar . . .

Footsteps on the path brought Him back to reality. Morning had come. "Master?" came a whisper.

It was John. Jesus looked up and smiled. "Good morning, John," He said as He stood up and grasped the other's hand. John smiled back.

Jesus turned to look at the rising sun, and His face reflected its glory. Breathing one last prayer for strength, He pivoted and headed back toward the city.

When He entered it He was greeted by a group of children. They clamored about Him on all sides as He made His way to the Temple. At least they accepted Him for who He was! By the time He reached the Temple a crowd had formed around Him, and He began to teach them there.

While He was teaching, some Pharisees and scribes approached Him. They had a woman with them. The group of men threw her at His feet. "Teacher," one of them said, "this woman was caught in the very act of adultery. Moses said in the law that such should be stoned to death. What do You say?"

Jesus knew *she* wasn't the one on trial. He was. She was merely a pawn in their scheme to trap Him. His heart filled with pity. Sighing, He knelt in the dirt beside her and began writing in the dust with His finger. The men grew impatient with His apparent delay and demanded an answer, so Jesus straightened and met them with a challenge. "Whichever one of you has committed no sin may throw the first stone."

He bent and continued writing in the dirt. One by one they peered over His shoulder then drifted away without looking back.

Finally, Jesus was alone with the woman. As she raised her head and looked into His face, a flood of memories washed across His mind. The black hair, the brown eyes, the tear-streaked face . . .

WHERE ARE YOUR ACCUSERS?

"Woman, where are your accusers?" He asked. "Is there no one here to condemn you?"

Timidly she looked around before replying, "No one, Lord." She whispered it again, unbelievingly, "No one."

"I don't accuse you either," He said as He helped her to her feet. "Go and sin no more."

She gazed into His face, her eyes brimming with thankfulness. The earthen jar He had given her in childhood could not compare with what He gave her now. She whispered her gratitude, then slowly walked away—transformed!

The loneliness and distress rolled from His shoulders as He watched her go. Seeing her joy and newness of life was like a fountain pouring into Him the strength He needed to go on. With renewed vigor, He turned again to the crowd that remained and continued teaching them there.

CHAPTER FOUR

Premonitions

Breezes blow. Great white clouds drift across a blue desert sky, followed by their shadow counterparts across the rough and barren wasteland. A hawk circles slowly overhead, swooping low now and then to catch rising eddies of air that the arid hills cast off in shimmering waves.

Walking slowly, a Figure appears upon the skyline. He pauses to watch the circling hawk. Moving again, His shoulders slightly stooped and with a slow yet deliberate stride, He walks on. Topping a rise, He hesitates as the breeze becomes wind, hurling sand wildly. Pulling His cloak about Him and squinting His eyes, He continues in the direction of a lone peak. Bending forward—head into the wind, hair blowing freely, clothes flapping—He moves up the steep slope, where He gratefully takes shelter behind a large summit rock.

Pulling His legs in against His chest, He sits with arms half-wrapped around His knees. Then letting His head fall back, He leans against the rock. The wind calms. His sky-turned eyes gaze into an infinite blue strewn with clouds.

The peaceful heavens are welcome relief to His tired city eyes. The clouds drift gently, unlike the frenzied movement of the teeming throngs in the city, where He walks alone in spite of being surrounded. People, yes, but still alone . . . always alone. Why?

Sighing deeply, He leans His forehead against His arms, letting His mind drift with the pure white clouds. He thinks of *them* . . . the city people, the seething, searching crowd—purposeless, pointless lives with little to live for and less to look forward to, except perhaps death.

Death is their only hope . . . *His* death. But they do not know that, nor do they care. And it is because none seem to care or understand that He must continue walking alone. Perhaps someday they will know, someday they will care, but just now . . .

His eyes wander across the rocky, gray-brown wasteland below the sky. Something attracts His attention. Protruding above a nearby pile of rocks, a small red flower grows upward. It reaches for the sun as though heaven provides its reason for living.

Looking closer, He notices the edges of petals that have begun to wrinkle and whither. There is little water here, where wind and heat constantly threaten a flower's existence. It *appears* as if the arid desert is slowly draining the life from this solitary plant.

Suddenly a smile smooths the careworn features of His leathered face, because beneath this small red flower He sees the tiny sprouts of seedlings that have been dropped. They are groping their way through the shadowy places, reaching upward for the sun.

As the sun sets and the twilight gathers, observe the solitary figure of a Man silhouetted against the evening sky, making His way back. Back down the desert slopes—back to the peopled city. Desert breezes ruffle His hair and clothes . . . and far on the distant horizon a hawk circles.

CHAPTER FIVE

My Friend Peter

Introductions

I have to tell you about Peter. Almost every one of his lessons he learned the hard way. But he learned. He's loyal through and through now. Sometimes his learning was hard on Me too, but never as hard as it was on him.

I can't reminisce about Peter without recalling the first time we met. I had just come to the lake with his brother Andrew and a friend named Philip. Andrew had tried to prepare Me by saying, "He really *is* a good man. On the inside he's gentle as a kitten."

Well, the cat he resembled most was a lion! It was early morning, and he was just returning from a night's fruitless fishing. Coming from Nazareth, I thought I'd heard every word in the book, but Andrew made the mistake of asking if it had been a bad catch. Peter used all *those* words and then some. When he finally ran out of breath, Andrew introduced us. Peter spat on the ground and sneered, "Well, Prophet, why don't You put some fish in our lake?"

"Go out again, and I'll come with you," I replied.

He stared at Me for what seemed hours. I didn't look away. "Get in," he finally muttered. So I did. Andrew and Philip did too.

He had a right to be skeptical. The fishermen of Galilee fish at night for a reason. The lake is so clear that fish can see the nets in daylight.

I waited till we were some ways offshore and then told them to cast their nets. Well, there were so many fish that the net broke, and then there was such a bustle of activity that I almost choked laughing. Peter hailed a passing boat, and we secured the catch with their nets. I guess it was a record catch for the lake. Peter just stared, with mouth agape, while it all sank in. Suddenly he threw himself down at My feet. "Depart from me," he said, "for I am a sinful man!"

Andrew was right about his brother! He *is* a good man.

What others might think never seemed to bother Peter. He always said what he felt. You never had to guess what he was thinking, and I like that! One time I asked all the disciples who the crowds thought I was. They told me all kinds of things, but when I asked who *they* thought I was, it got real quiet. They were embarrassed by the silence, and I could feel their awkwardness. It was obvious that no one wanted to actually admit before the others that he thought I was the Son of God. No one, that is, except Peter. He suddenly exploded, "You are *the Christ,* the Son of the living God!"

I loved him for that, because it told me that, despite his impulsive, assertive, blundering ways, Peter was letting my Father work in his life. That sort of response is not natural to flesh and blood!

You know, the difference between blundering Peter and polished Judas was that Peter didn't let his defects come between us. He clung to Me as tenaciously as a vine to its arbor, even when he felt most unworthy. Sometimes he seems like a contradiction in terms. Like that time he said "Depart from me, for I am a sinful man" while clinging to My feet.

Some would say it was a contradiction for him to tell Me I must not go to Jerusalem shortly after he had declared I was God's Son. But it really wasn't contradictory. His intentions were good despite his confusion. When I rebuked Satan for inspiring that thought, the pain on Peter's face was almost too much for Me. It was like his best friend had just slapped him in the face. I wanted to throw My arms around him then and there, but I prayed for him. My Father knows how much I have prayed for him!

I remember that at Capernaum a cluster of Pharisees pulled him aside and asked whether I paid the Temple tax. Of all the disciples, you would have expected *him* to know the right answer. Why, just a short time before, as I mentioned, he had acknowledged Me as the Son of God. Every Jew knows that as long as we have been a nation, prophets and holy men have been exempted from the Temple tax. I'm sure he meant well and did not see the trap, because he loudly asserted that I was as loyal a Jew as the next guy and would certainly pay.

He came into the house and smugly informed me he had "just taken care of that pious delegation!"

I said, "Peter, whom do kings tax—their children or their subjects?"

"Their subjects," he replied.

All the wind left his sail when I pointed out, "Then the children are free, aren't they?"

Crestfallen, he turned to go and try to straighten things out with the crafty priests, but I had an idea and sent him to the lake for the answer. He came back as excited as a child at Hanukkah and said, "You should have seen their expressions when I pulled that coin from the fish's mouth! I guess we showed them, didn't we, Master."

"Yes, Peter, *we* sure did."

More Miracles

Oh, it's great to think back on it all! I remember one particular Sabbath in Capernaum when I was staying at Peter's house. His mother-in-law was sick. In fact, she was almost delirious with a terribly high fever. Peter's wife had died, you know, and you could tell he had loved her by the way he cared for her mother. Things did not look good! Peter epitomized the word "anxious." I wanted to help, so I healed her. It made the whole Sabbath extra-special to see the change of expression on his face when the fever left her!

But Peter wasn't too good at keeping secrets. In fact, he wasn't too good at keeping quiet about anything. This was no exception, and soon all Capernaum had heard of the cure. As soon as the sun went down, I think every sick or crippled person in town found their way to Peter's house. It was so crowded that one crippled man had his friends lower him through a hole they made in the roof. Oh, you should have seen Peter's face when the plaster began to fall! "My house, my house!" he screamed. "What are you doing to my house?"

There was really no cause to worry. I fixed the cripple, and he and his friends fixed the roof. We were up late that night! I just couldn't say no to even one sufferer. The last one didn't leave till close to 2:00 in the morning. I got up at 5:00 a.m. to spend some time with my Father. Peter and the others slept in, but I prayed for them that their strength might fail not.

On the Lake

You must have heard about that night on the lake. Actually, there were two nights worth mentioning. The first took place after a particularly long day. I was so exhausted that I couldn't stay awake, so shortly after we were under sail I lay down in the bow of the boat. There is nothing quite as relaxing as the motion of a boat on water, and almost immediately I was asleep for the night. I must have been sleeping soundly, too, because the next thing I knew, Peter was shaking Me and screaming at the top of his lungs.

It seems that a storm had risen, and we were being blown about. I'll never forget how beautiful the lightning was against that dark and cloudy sky. I was actually enjoying the brisk air and invigorating spray, but the others were in a panic.

I stood up and said to the storm, "Peace, be still!" My Father took care of the rest, and moments later the moon shimmered a path across the mirrored surface of Galilee. My friends just sat in dumb disbelief. They *should* have known there was nothing to fear. Even Peter was speechless.

I said there were two nights worth mentioning. Here's what happened during the other one. It had been another unusually long day. In fact, we had ended it by feeding more than 20,000 people. Everyone got pretty excited about that meal, and I guess they wanted to make a big deal over Me because of it. They called it a miracle feast, but it was the same power those farmers see at work in their fields every day. I guess they don't consider a thing miraculous unless it happens quickly.

Anyway, I declined the honors and had to insist that everyone go home. My closest friends were pretty upset, so I sent them out on the lake. I hoped that an evening on the water would settle and soothe their spirits. It's so quiet and peaceful out there! I stayed behind and climbed the hillside to a favorite overlook of mine, where I could watch the moonlight on the water. As the stars wheeled past overhead, I talked with My Father, and I have to say that if there's something more settling than a night on the lake, it's talking to Him.

While I was talking and listening, a wind came up. I suppose gale would be a better choice of words, for it tossed my friends' boat about like a cork. I could see them from where I sat. The storm was good for them. They had talked themselves into a deep depression and needed something to divert their troubled minds. For about six hours they bailed and rowed against contrary winds. Finally, they gave themselves up for lost, and then the timing was right for Me to help.

As you know, with My Father nothing is impossible. I set out walking toward them on the water. At first they didn't realize what they were really seeing because the waves kept hiding us from full view of each other, but as I got closer, their minds were seized with unparalleled fear. They dropped their oars and sat frozen in mute terror. The wind was flailing My hair and robe about, and I guess they thought I was an apparition. They began thinking they were either dead men or soon to be such.

I shouted through the gale, "It's all right! Don't be afraid! It's Me!"

This took a moment to sink in, and I began to walk as though I would pass them. Suddenly it all came together for Peter, and he grabbed the mast as he leaped to his feet and shouted, "If it's really You, let me come out to meet You!"

So I told him to come ahead, and with faith soaring he literally jumped from the boat. (Always the impulsive one!) It was great. You have never seen anyone as excited! He began running toward Me with the energy of a colt in a spring pasture. Then he turned around to see if everyone else was watching, and when he looked back toward Me again, a wave came between us, blocking his view. I chose that moment to let him slowly start sinking. To say he panicked would be putting it mildly! Just before his head went under, I came back into view, and he screamed, "Lord, save me!"

I grabbed his upstretched hand and walked with him to the boat. If you've ever seen a puppy cower fearfully with its tail between its legs, then you'll know how poor Peter looked as he sat there cold and wet. If only he had learned then that he was secure only as long as he kept his focus on Me. If only they all had learned that!

Mount Hermon

During the late summer of My thirty-third year, we traveled north from Galilee, past Caesarea, to the base of Mount Hermon. For as long as I can remember, I have loved the mountains! Nazareth is a mountain town, and from atop the slopes above our woodshop, I used to gaze westward across the blue vastness of the Mediterranean.

The peaks surrounding Nazareth were seldom higher than 3,000 feet, but looking north from their summits, I could see the snowfields of Hermon. It is over three times the height of our mountains and seems to belong more to the sky than the earth. I felt a strange kinship to that mountain, and I longed to climb it.

It was late afternoon as we approached the base. We had been walking through dust and heat since midmorning, but cool downslope winds told of the snowfields and rarified air that we knew were higher. I felt new energy, and My desire to climb would not be postponed till morning. Most of My friends were weary and decided to make camp, but Peter and the two Zebedee brothers shared My eagerness to press on. The mountain was calling us, and we had to go.

We were more than halfway up by the time the sun began going down. It cast lengthy shadows before us as the mountain warmed to gold. Sunset was glorious! The snowfields, reflecting sunlight, shimmered all the brightness of the day into one grand shower of diamond sparks! We stopped to rest and gaze as twilight settled down like a mist of lavender and a powder of rose. No one spoke.

I don't know how long we sat lost in contemplation, but it was long enough for our weary muscles to begin setting up. It took determined efforts to continue, but we finally reached the summit in darkness and exhaustion. The others were soon asleep.

I could have put My finger on a star. I felt close to home there, and I spent the next several hours talking with My Father. One of the things I asked Him for was to somehow give Peter, James, and John a glimpse of the glory that was Mine before the world began.

In answer, He sent two from the world of light, and the glory that accompanied them made the sunset pale to insignificance. It's hard to describe what followed, but I remember My friends waking up and trying to shield their eyes. It was one of those rare times when Peter was at a loss for words.

Usually he was first to speak, and sometimes his words seemed to precede his thoughts. After My guests had returned to heaven, Peter finally broke the silence by blurting out, "Master, it was good for us to be here! Let's make three tabernacles here; one for You and one for Moses and one for Elijah."

Tabernacles! Those are shelters the pilgrims build when they come for Succoth. As if Moses and Elijah would leave heaven to take up residence on Mount Hermon! I had to laugh.

About then a brilliant cloud hovered over our heads, and My Father spoke. You should have seen Peter! He hit the ground facedown like a dead man, throwing his arms over his head and shaking as though he expected to be struck by lightning. I reassured him and the others, but he didn't speak again until we had almost finished descending the mountain.

Last Days

Perhaps the thing I appreciate most about Peter is how quickly he repents when he knows he has been wrong. So many of My followers think they need to let My Father cool down before they can return after sinning. They should take a lesson from My friend Peter. He didn't let anything keep him away for long! And he didn't do anything halfway, either. He put his whole heart into whatever he did, right or wrong!

There was the time that night we celebrated Passover in the upper room. "You will never wash *my* feet!" he said, but moments later he was just as earnestly begging Me to wash his whole body after I told him what the symbol said about our relationship.

Peter's instruction was not yet complete. The hardest lesson of his life came later that same Passover night. I would have saved him if I could, but he was so headstrong and self-assured that there was nothing I could do. I tried to warn him. I told him he would deny Me that very night, but he didn't hear. He didn't seem to be listening when I said I would pray for him so that his strength would not fail, but that didn't prevent Me from praying. I knew that when he was converted again, he would strengthen his brothers.

We left the upper room and headed toward a favorite spot of Mine in the Garden of Gethsemane. Upon reaching the garden, Peter, James, John, and I left the others and went a bit farther. I asked them to wait and pray near a small grove of olive trees, while I went over to a nearby rock that was bathed in moonlight.

The next few hours were the hardest of My life. The time was at hand when I was to be betrayed, mocked, and crucified. Everything within Me resisted the idea of death. I pleaded for another way, but it seemed Heaven could not hear Me. I had never felt so alone!

I went back to where My three closest friends were. I wanted someone to talk to, someone to listen, but they were all sleeping. I must have looked as bad as I felt, because when I woke them, they were frightened and didn't recognize Me at first. When I told them that I felt like I was dying, they sat up and said they would pray for Me. Encouraged, I left them there and went back to the rock. I felt better just knowing they were praying too.

Some time later I came back to where they were and found them sleeping again. Peter had told Me earlier that he would go with Me to death, so I tried to rouse him to ask if he couldn't stay awake with Me for just one hour. He only mumbled something about cold and dark, then turned over and continued sleeping. I know he would have wanted to stay awake had he realized how badly I needed him, but he was just a man, and he was weak. So was I.

I stumbled back to the rock. I pleaded and cried for another way, but there was no answer. It's impossible for Me to tell you just how difficult the struggle was! At one time I was almost to the point of giving up when I thought of Peter and how Satan had desired to have him—and not him only, but all My friends, the whole human race.

I saw the pain and suffering of a world without hope. I saw blood-drenched battlefields strewn with dying. I saw parents grieving for children who were no more. I saw children grieving because their parents would not stay together. I saw endless disease, poverty, slavery, and oppression; the living and dying, weeping and groaning of a world in darkness. I saw the burdens and the burdened of all the ages, and it was enough. Satan desired them all, but they were not his. I determined to reclaim Peter . . . and the world!

I fell dying to the ground then, and My Father, My dear Father, sent help—a messenger from the world of light. He lifted Me up and showed Me the future results of My death. I was saddened to see that many of the human race would not take the hope offered, but I also saw the redeemed as they stepped through the gates to My Father's house. I saw their gladness and heard their rejoicing. I saw Peter rush to meet and embrace Me, and I was strengthened. It would be worth it all! The ransom price was not too great to pay.

The messenger departed, and refreshed, I returned once more to My sleeping friends. I stood for some time looking down at that precious sleeping group. I think I know how a mother feels when she gazes on her sleeping children. The world was waiting for them, and they seemed so vulnerable, so inexperienced. *Let them sleep on,* I thought. *They'll need rest. There are great things in store for them and much to be done. These 11, with their friends, will turn the world—and Satan's kingdom—upside down!*

The mob arrived, and the nightmare began. Peter woke with a start and went into immediate action, cutting off an ear. He seemed so confused when I restored the ear to its owner! Like a rabbit at night when surprised by a ray of light, he hesitated, trying to decide whether to freeze or run. He chose to run, and hollering at the other disciples to save themselves, he bolted into the night.

I didn't see him again until after My preliminary trial before Annas. He had cautiously made his way back and was mingling with a group around a fire. He didn't know I was watching. Some soldiers formed a circle around Me and began shoving Me about. They put an old feed bag over My head, and I lost sight of Peter, but there was no mistaking his voice. He was shouting vehemently that he did not know Me. They began hitting Me in the face and head and threw punches at My ribs and stomach.

One blow caught Me in the mouth, and I felt blood running from My lips. Someone ripped the bag from My head and whirled Me around. He raised a fist, but for one brief moment, through a gap in the crowd, I saw Peter, shouting across the fire at someone who was laughing and pointing at him.

Our eyes met. He paused in midbreath, and then the fist struck Me full in the face. When My vision cleared, Peter was gone.

You probably know most of what happened after that. The trial, Caiaphas, Herod, Pilate, the floggings, the nails, the cross. Through it all, that last look in Peter's eyes kept coming back to Me. I don't think I have ever seen eyes express pain and sorrow any more than his did then. I knew he was sorry, and I wanted terribly to go to him, but it was impossible. I wanted to find him and tell him that it was all right, tell him that *everything was going to be all right!*

Glorious Morning

The nightmare finally faded to blackness and was finished. The next thing I remember, it was morning! I awoke to blazing light and knew that We had won! Angels were everywhere, and the singing and the glory were beyond words! Gabriel shouted, "Your Father calls You!" I folded the graveclothes and stepped out into wonder.

It took a minute for it all to sink in. Angels and other friends from home were all around, embracing Me and saying I had been victorious. Everyone wanted to talk at once. Oh, it was a glorious reunion! The angels were trying to hurry Me off somewhere when I remembered Peter. I asked the two nearest Me if they would tell My disciples—and Peter—that I would go ahead of them to Galilee and meet them there. Then I thought of Mary.

Mary is another story, and I *must* tell it to you later. Mary would be coming to the grave, and I just had to stay by to meet her. I'm so glad I did; she needed Me. Just before I left, I gave her the same message for the disciples and Peter.

Homecoming followed, and it was the best! My Father rushed out to meet Me and shouted to everyone, "Rejoice, My Son is home again!" Words fail, but there is a homecoming planned for you, too, and soon you'll know just how good it is.

It wasn't easy to pull Myself away, but I told My Father that I needed to be away for a little while. There was something I really wanted to do. He gave Me a hug and said that We'd have lots of time when I got back. He is the source of selflessness!

I couldn't wait till Galilee to see Peter again. When he left the trial, he had gone to Gethsemane, to the very rock at which I had prayed. My Father told Me that Peter had been praying to die. Mary got My message to him, and he raced all the way to My empty tomb. When he didn't find Me there, he returned, crestfallen, to Gethsemane. That is where I found him.

He was as overjoyed to see Me, as I was to see him! We clung to each other like friends who have been long separated. I'll not share all we talked about during the next couple of hours. They were special, private, meaningful, and we parted without sadness!

I just have to tell you one more thing about Peter. When I went to meet the disciples at Galilee, they were out fishing in Peter's boat. It was early, before sunrise. They had fished all night and caught nothing. A low fog hung over the lake, and I called through the mist, "Children, have you any meat?"

When they answered "No!" I told them to cast their nets on My side of their boat, which they did. No sooner had they cast than there was a great catch. John shouted, "It's the Lord!" and Peter dived in to swim for shore.

I had to laugh! His enthusiasm reminded Me of a waggy-tailed pup I once had. Good old Peter! His impulsiveness hadn't changed much, but he had. He was as solid as a rock now, and loyal through and through. One day he would die for Me, and at the last minute impulsively ask to be crucified head down. But that would not be the end of the story; it would actually be the real beginning. You see, I have a throne with his name on it and a home waiting for him . . .

Maybe I'll tell you one thing we talked about during those two hours in Gethsemane. I have an appointment to keep. Peter and I are going sailing on the sea of glass!

CHAPTER SIX

sonrise—
while
the city slept

"Jesus went unto the Mount of Olives. And early in the morning he came again into the temple" (John 8:1, 2).

Gingerly planting His bare feet on the cold stone floor, He rises and begins dressing, careful lest He should wake the other members of the yet sleeping household. Stepping into a pair of sandals, He reaches for His outer garment, then quietly opens the door and moves out into the darkness.

The stars, twinkling remotely in the black sky, do not betray the imminence of dawn. As He makes His way through the city, He thinks of the throngs of people who will soon fill the now quiet streets. Day after day He has walked among them and with them, seeking to befriend the friendless, to comfort the lonely, and to help wherever possible. Day after day He has walked and worked in loneliness; always in the midst of crowds, yet somehow still alone . . . so far from home.

He reaches the outskirts of the city now and continues walking, descending through fields and pastures toward a valley below the city. Walking. He has walked much during the past few years. Driven by a burden for humanity, He has moved from city to city—encouraging, listening, understanding, bringing hope. Yet little *human* encouragement offers consolation to His weary heart. True, a handful seem to appreciate His efforts . . . appreciate

Him. But even they do not *really* understand.

Crossing the valley, He begins to ascend the mountain on the other side. The mountain. How often He has come here! How often He has enjoyed the beauty that abounds here! His steps slow as the path steepens, yet He is scarcely aware of physical exertion, for He is consumed by a burden that weighs upon His heart—a burden to see the complete happiness of those around Him. This is His joy. But He seems so alone in His efforts to help. Always alone. It is at times such as this when He especially longs for the companionship of others . . . if only one other. Another who appreciates. Another to understand, to offer encouragement.

A great weariness seems almost to overwhelm Him. If only . . . He lurches forward, stumbling over an unnoticed rock in the path and falls to the ground. No one but the birds behold His prostrate form. No one witnesses His struggle to rise and then fall again, as though toiling under an overwhelming load.

Perspiration such as no exertion ever caused mingles with tears in finding its way down His face, where it falls upon the grass that cushions His head. Early-morning dew casts a damp cover, as if nature weeps with Him, sharing the mental anguish that oppresses this lonely, human form.

Gasping as one who runs a long race, He buries His face in the grass, arms outstretched on the cold ground. His fingers dig slowly into the sod. Clutching handfuls of moist soil, He pulls Himself to His knees and with a voice barely audible says, "Father. Oh, My Father."

Only the trees see the crumpled Figure with bowed head. Only the hushed songbirds hear the sobs that pour from His very soul. And only nature witnesses as peace settles upon the kneeling form.

As the rich colors of purple, crimson, and gold bathe the mountaintop in resplendent glory, a Figure is silhouetted against the dawn. Standing alone, the world's Redeemer pauses for a moment, gazing upon the still-sleeping city below, then begins walking *back*, strengthened for another day.

CHAPTER SEVEN

Greenpeace

Purchases are consummated with the clank and clatter of exchanged coins as shrewd merchants and haggling buyers add to the bustle of the market. Livestock voice stubborn resistance as herdsmen mutter and curse. Everywhere jostling throngs of purposeful travelers are bent on accomplishing some errand of busy import. Above the din, scribes and Pharisees engage in loud debate. Occasionally a blast of a trumpet clears the path so one with rank or nobility can make his celebrated movement through town. Beggars and cripples cry out for alms.

Through this bustling lakeside, teeming with its smells and sounds of activity, a Man moves calmly toward a docked boat and its cargo of waiting fishermen.

"I'm sorry to have kept you waiting," He says, swinging aboard the small vessel. "I stopped to talk with Mary. She seemed discouraged when I saw her last. But now let's be off! I'm as eager as you to finally be under way."

"*That's* for sure!" responds Peter. "I fear for my nerves if we don't find some peace and quiet soon. It's not that I don't like people, You understand, but most seem to be little more than curiosity seekers."

"It's true, Peter. Many of them do come only out of curiosity. I also wish there were more earnest ones among them." The Latecomer pauses, contemplation softening His careworn brow, then adds, "But whoever comes, I will in no way cast out."

A moment of quiet follows, full of wonderings. Then James abruptly changes the subject. "What bearing shall we take? The lake is large, and there are many possibilities."

"Well, James," comes the reply, "I vote for the northeast shore. It's peaceful and quiet there, and this time of year Mount Hermon's snowy slopes will make a beautiful backdrop to the blue and green of spring."

"Then bend the oars, men," cries James (whose boat it is), "and soon we will be catching sun as well as carp or barbels along one of the finest bits of shoreline on Galilee."

So time flew, as it always does when a happy purpose occupies the day. These fishermen were eager to ply their trade, and the Teacher, for such was the Latecomer, looked forward to a space of uncrowded time with His men.

Eagerly He joins them, muscles straining at the oars, as they dip rhythmically and pull across the placid reflection that is Galilee. But word of mouth is often the quickest means of travel, and so it happens that news flashes from farm to farm and town to town along the northeasterly direction in which their boat is moving. Judging by the interest with which this boat's progress is noted and passed along, one would judge the Teacher to be quite popular. He is!

The rowers approach the green velvet hills composing the northern shore. One by one the oars abruptly cease their circular motion. The men gaze in wonder at the majestic snow-clad slopes of Hermon. As they watch, great white clouds that have been obscuring the mountain melt into blue, revealing the summit. Reflected sunlight glistens from the mountain's icefields and leaps again from the mirrored surface of the lake. The men drink in the scene, filling their souls with energy and peace. Pressures drop away like weighted nets into the lake, and their voices mingle in glad expressions of joy and wonder. The next few days will be greatly appreciated and well-deserved!

Turning from Hermon, they look at the Teacher and discover Him gazing in a different direction. Silently, chin cradled upon hugged knees, He looks across the liquid surface. He appears lost in thought, and their eyes follow the direction of His gaze. Suddenly their holiday vanishes and is replaced by a noisy crowd expectantly thronging the shoreline.

The men suggest turning about and looking for a more inaccessible shoreline. The Teacher looks at His disappointed companions, at the hopeful crowd, and then back again. His lips move silently, as if in prayer, and then with a careworn smile He gestures toward the shore, saying, "Friends, welcome to the blue and green of spring."

He taught them there. He healed their diseases. He broke bread for them. And His friends remembered that He had said, "Whoever comes to Me, I will in no way cast out!"

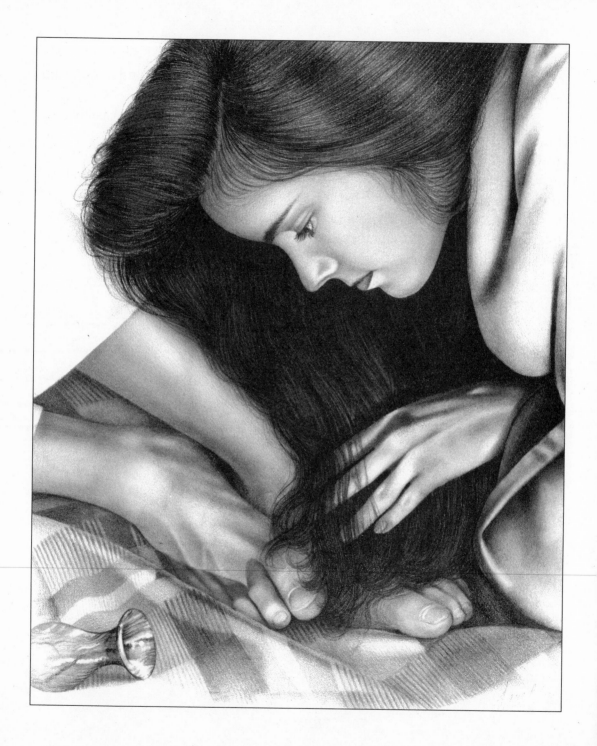

CHAPTER EIGHT

At His Feet

Life Before

Oh, I've seen Him. I've seen Him many times as He passed by with crowds on every side. I remember the first time He passed by. It was hard, to be sure, but it seemed as if He had paused to look right at me. I'll never forget His eyes!

Have you ever seen eyes brimming with love and melting with understanding? I have! His eyes were so deep with compassion that I had to look away, and He passed by. When I looked again, the only reminder of His passing was an eddy of dust settling upon the road.

He always seemed to be so busy, so sought after, so in demand, that I despaired of ever seeing Him again. You must understand that though my line of work provided many a customer, I was seldom welcome at any social gathering. When I wasn't working, I was usually alone.

Curiously, though He was always surrounded by people, yet it seemed to me as if He also felt alone. There was a look about Him of one who does not belong. If you looked closely, you could detect just a hint of sadness in His eyes and the slightest stoop in His broad shoulders. You got the feeling that He lived and walked with some secret sorrow or hidden knowledge that was always just beyond the shadows. Though my loneliness was for different reasons, still I felt that He was a kindred spirit. I wanted to see Him again.

There was something about His eyes that attracted me. I wondered whether they were His Father's or His mother's eyes. They seemed to follow me into dreams, and often I would awaken with a feeling that He was near. Strange how He can feel near even when He isn't in town!

I determined to discover where I might find Him, but those whom I asked caused me to feel as though He would have no time for a woman like me. They said He was a prophet, a holy man, a religious leader. And of course, everyone knows that religious leaders have little or no time for common sinners like me. I had learned that lesson well from the leading Pharisee in Bethany!

Years before, I had lived in Bethany. In fact, I was born there. My parents died when I was still a child. Fortunately, I have an older brother who was able to work and provide for my sister and me. His work took him away from our home for long hours every day, but he never complained.

My sister was often gone also. She was very active in community affairs, especially church-related ones. There was always another project to keep her busy, so I was often home alone.

I've never believed in making excuses. I blame no one but myself for it, but complications arose when I began receiving a visitor while home alone. He was that Pharisee I mentioned, and we became involved in sin. It didn't continue long, but it left me devastated! I was filled with remorse and burdened by guilt. When I went to the synagogue in search of peace and forgiveness, Simon made it clear that I was not welcome there.

He further told me that there had been nothing between us and that should I ever tell anyone there had, he would emphatically deny it. He was a man of reputation and influence, and he convinced me that I would be the one who suffered if ever I accused him of immorality. He then suggested that it would be best for *him* if I left town.

This was really a double rejection. Simon had no time or use for me, and as the religious leader he made me feel distanced from God, as well. My sense of loneliness was overwhelming! If I had suddenly been stricken with leprosy, I could not have felt more rejected.

For a time I remained in Bethany, but my situation did not improve. I felt unclean and uncomfortable around most people, especially my old friends. When I attended the synagogue, I'd wonder whether anyone else knew my guilty secret. If someone looked in my direction at the market or the town well, I felt as though they could see right through me. I avoided eye contact and anyone familiar.

Things became tense and awkward at home. My brother and sister knew something was wrong and tried to get me to talk about it, but I refused. I would rather have died than for them to know what sort of failure I had made of my life. My sleep left me, and I often spent whole nights awake. I must have cried a riverful of tears!

Finally, one night I decided to leave. I gathered what few belongings I could carry and slipped away without goodbyes. I wasn't exactly sure where to go. All I knew was that I wanted to leave everything and everyone familiar and start over.

I walked the short distance down the mountain to Jerusalem, getting there just as they were opening the eastern gate. The capital was too big and too busy for me. Besides, it was close enough to home that I feared running into someone who knew me.

I spent the next few weeks drifting northward along the road to Shechem. I did odd jobs along the way and managed to keep food in my stomach, but I couldn't seem to escape the emptiness in my heart. I passed through Nain and considered living in Nazareth, but finally settled in the Galilean lake town of Magdala.

Things started out OK at first. I got a job at a small eatery, working as a dishwasher and cook's assistant. The pay wasn't much, but I took meals free and managed to make my rent. A few months after I started working there, the local economy took a drop, and business slowed to the point that I lost my job.

I tried unsuccessfully to find other work, and I came into great want.

My landlord served me an eviction notice, and I didn't know what I was going to do. Tearfully I begged for more time to come up with the rent, but he seemed indifferent to my pleas. He told me that even men couldn't find work in our town. He said there was no chance that I would find a job sufficient to pay the rent. And then he proposed an arrangement whereby I might stay rent-free.

At first I rejected His proposition, but he told me to think about it for a couple of days and consider if it were not better than the alternative of sleeping on the street. I'm ashamed to admit it, but I accepted the arrangement he offered. I felt that my past was already so tainted that it was pointless to be concerned about chastity. It would have been far better to have slept on the street.

Things went from bad to worse! Apparently he told some of his friends about our "arrangement," and soon others came knocking at my door. I thought to discourage their purpose by asking a large sum of money. To my surprise and regret, many agreed to the price, and though I soon became quite wealthy, my self-worth could not have been poorer. I suffered regular and great depressions, often wishing that I might die.

And then one day He passed by again. I heard the noisy commotion of a large crowd and went to my window. He was there—in the center of the crowd—and they were headed toward the lake. I grabbed a shawl and hurried after them. It wasn't enough to see Him from afar. If He was going to say something, I wanted to hear it.

We stopped on a grassy hillside that sloped gently into Galilee. Like a great swarm of bees, we settled down among the flowers and greenery of spring. He was standing on the lakeshore. From where we sat, reflected sunlight in the water at His back created a halo effect about Him that added to our feelings of expectation. A stillness spread over the crowd, and then He spoke.

Oh, how I treasure the things He said! Such things as "Come to me all you who are weary and overburdened, and I will give you rest." "Peace I give to you; my peace I leave with you. I don't give the way the world does." Don't let your heart be troubled, neither let it be afraid." "Whoever comes to me I will never cast out."

I listened spellbound to words that were like water to my parched soul. The picture of God that He gave me was in sharp contrast to the one I had received from other religious leaders. For a long time after He had finished talking, I lingered by, waiting for an opportunity to talk to Him. Finally He turned to me, and in His eyes I saw the same welcome that His words had made me feel. I fell on the ground at His feet as words and tears came gushing from me.

Through bitter sobs I told Him the dark, ugly secrets of my life. He listened without condemnation, and when I was finished, He knelt on the ground beside me and prayed strong prayers in my behalf. I felt my guilt and uncleanliness drop away from me like the leaves of autumn. The winter in my life was over. Springtime had come.

Transformation

Well, Jesus passed on to other towns, other people, but I stayed in Magdala. Perhaps staying wasn't such a good idea, for the same old friends and clients kept coming around. It wasn't long before I found myself involved again in the life I had thought to leave behind. The old burden of guilt returned, along with its accompanying sleeplessness and regrets. I longed for peace and wished that Jesus lived in Magdala so that I could go to Him for help.

I heard that He was teaching at the north end of the lake, in Capernaum, so one morning I set out to find Him. It wasn't difficult. When I got to the town I saw a crowd gathered on the beach. Joining them, I discovered that Jesus was teaching from a fishing boat anchored just off shore.

He was telling a story about a wayward son who journeyed to a far country and became involved in a life of sin. How I could relate to the misery that boy felt as he fed pigs and thought of home! When Jesus pictured God rushing out to meet the returning prodigal, my heart leaped within me. There was even hope for people who knowingly became involved in sin. There was hope for me!

After His talk was over and the crowd had gone home, I found myself at Jesus' feet once more. Again I heard His prayers in my behalf and felt the prodigal's joy in belonging to the family.

Sadly, I have to tell you that my joy was short-lived. I returned to Magdala and my life of sin. But the good news is that Jesus never gave up on me. During the next few months our paths continued to cross. Five more times I came into His presence, and each time I knew His welcome and forgiveness.

In His presence there is comfort! In His presence there is peace. And I finally determined to stay in His presence. There was a sort of inner circle, composed of several men and a number of women who traveled with Him. Two of the women, Joanna and Susanna, invited me to join them in ministering to Jesus of their substance. And so it was that I became a follower of Jesus.

In the days and weeks that followed, I began to understand more about those eyes of His. They were His Father's eyes! And His Father was none other than our very God! He had come to show us what God is like, come to remove the veil that dimmed our view. Eternity had stepped into time so that we might understand.

He told us of the Father with stories that I'll never forget. I saw the Father planting a vineyard and doing all possible for its growth. I saw Him preparing a wedding feast with a guest list that left out no one. On the darkest night, the Father was out looking for lost sheep. At midnight He was helping a neighbor in need. He was the king who made the common man His friend. I saw the Father rushing to welcome a wayward son. I saw Him giving *His* Son so that all who would believe might live forever.

Jesus made the picture so clear! Just seeing Jesus made me feel as though I had seen the Father. God loved through Jesus' eyes and words. I began to understand where the love came from as I watched Him. He would rise a great while before day and go out to some solitary place where He would pray. No matter how late He had gone to sleep or how tired He had been the night before, He always kept that appointment. Sometimes He would even spend entire nights in prayer and come forth refreshed and strengthened for another day.

He and the Father were one, and I began to understand that I too could have a close relationship with His Father. In fact, He once said that the whole basis of eternal life is in knowing God. At first I had difficulty believing that the sovereign God could be interested in spending time with someone like me. But as I watched Him in His Son, I knew it was true. Jesus mingled and mixed with common, everyday people, fisher folk by the sea, farmers in the field, women at the well.

The Pharisees thought that they slandered Him when they said "He eats with publicans and sinners," but to me they were speaking precious truth! God became man and sat at table with sinners!

I would have loved to have stayed with Him indefinitely. Sitting at His feet and listening to His words was my highest joy, but I wanted to go back to Bethany. I wanted to tell my family and friends what I had found, so one day I said goodbye to Joanna and the others and set out for home.

Home Again

I'll never forget the day I returned. As I neared Bethany, old familiar landmarks brought back all sorts of fond memories. I smiled while passing a large rock where I remembered playing "king of the mountain" with my brother and sister.

Thinking how good it would be to see my old loved ones and friends, I approached the gate in the western wall. Suddenly my recollections were interrupted by the cries of a nearby leper.

You must understand that our people believe leprosy to be a judgment for terrible sin. Anyone who got it had to leave home and family and was forced to advertise His calamity and sinfulness by calling out "Unclean, unclean!" Whether king or commoner, it made no difference—all were outcasts.

There was something in the voice of the one crying that seemed vaguely familiar. I cast a look in His direction, and my eyes verified what my ears could not believe. It was Simon! He was ghastly to look upon! The disease had made fearful inroads on his face and hands. I shuddered and gathered my shawl tighter about my head and shoulders. Trying to forget, I hurried through the gate.

I entered our home without knocking. Delicious odors told me I would find Martha in the kitchen. She was so startled to see me that she dropped the grinding stone she had been using, and it fell loudly to the floor. Lazarus rushed in from the next room to see if everything was all right, and oh, how it was! We laughed and cried and hugged each other, all trying to talk at once. It was wonderful to be back home!

To my joy, I discovered that Jesus had been through Bethany and that Martha and Lazarus had also gotten to know Him. Lazarus, in particular, had spent much time with Jesus, and they had become good friends. In fact, they told me that whenever Jesus passed through Bethany, He always stayed overnight or at least took meals in our home.

Not too long after I returned home, Jesus again came through our town. He was coming from the Temple in Jerusalem, where our religious leaders had twice tried to kill Him for claiming God as His father. The twelve were with Him, and though our home is small, Martha thought it would be special to have them all over for dinner. It was!

I should have been more of a help to Martha in the kitchen, but my *Friend*, whom they had tried to kill, was in our living room, and I just had to be near Him. The twelve and Lazarus more than filled the room, but I found a place on the floor near Jesus' feet and listened to Him there.

I'm not sure why, perhaps it's because that is where I first knelt and poured out my heart, but there's something about being near His feet that is special to me. Those feet, so tireless on journeys of love and ministry, were the feet of God. Sitting or kneeling before Him there was the highest honor, the highest privilege, I knew.

He said some things that day that worried me. Though the leaders at Jerusalem had not had their way with Him, He told us that the time would come when they would. He said that He would be betrayed into their hands and that they would deliver Him over to the Gentiles, who would mock, scourge, and finally crucify Him.

The dinner and talk ended far too quickly, and soon they were gone. Not long after they left, Lazarus became sick. At first we thought it was just an ordinary fever or flu, but his temperature climbed higher and higher. It got so high that he became delirious. Our concern grew!

We learned that after Jesus had left Bethany, He had gone through Jericho and on to the Jordan River. It was some 80 miles to where He was, but things were looking bad for Lazarus, so we sent a messenger to tell the Lord that our brother was sick. We knew He would come.

About a week later the messenger returned with news that this sickness was not unto death. We took courage, but the fever persisted. Martha and I took turns sitting by his bed and bathing Lazarus' brow. Now and then his mind would clear, and when it did we'd repeat the message from Jesus and assure him that everything was going to be OK.

Then Lazarus died. We didn't understand. We had not expected it to turn out like that. It was hard! Oh, how we wished Jesus had come, for sickness and death cannot remain in His presence.

We wrapped our brother's body in the customary graveclothes and placed Him in a rock-hewn tomb just outside of town. As the massive stone covering rolled heavily into place, the finality of our loss was almost overwhelming. I think my heart would have broken, but somehow (it is hard to explain) I felt as if Jesus' heart of love reached across the rocky miles and sustained me. Even though He was not in town, still I felt His presence and was comforted.

Then He came! Four days after we had buried our brother, He came. Oh, when Jesus comes, everything is all right! His Father's eyes spilled over as He listened to our grief, and then a most wonderful thing happened. He called out to Lazarus, and Lazarus *heard!* Our brother, *who had been dead, was alive again!*

At His Feet

Amid the noise and celebration at the tomb, Jesus quietly slipped away.

When we turned to thank Him, He could not be found. I discovered later that He had passed through Bethany's western gate and happened upon Simon.

As Jesus came into view, Simon had been mournfully crying, "Unclean, unclean." I guess he recognized Jesus as the *miracle worker*, but dismissed the idea of appealing for restoration, believing that the secret of his past placed him beyond the reach of a holy man.

For some reason, Jesus seems unable to pass by lepers without stopping. Perhaps it's because lepers are believed to be suffering for sin, and He had said that He'd come to set the captives free. At any rate, Jesus turned aside to touch Simon, and he was made whole. The healing of his soul came later.

Simon had always believed you get what you pay for and you pay for what you get. A *gift* of healing was more than he could take without somehow endeavoring to earn his way. For some time he struggled to find a way to repay Jesus, then one day Simon arrived at our door with a request.

He proposed to give a dinner in Jesus' honor. His plan was to invite the great and near great from miles around to a lavish feast at which Jesus would have the highest seat. He asked my sister to cater the meal, and he asked Lazarus to attend. He felt certain that having one who had been in the grave as guest would ensure attendance like no one around Jerusalem had ever seen. I was not invited.

Oh, how I wanted to attend! I couldn't forget that Jesus had predicted that He would die at the hands of His enemies, and I had a terrible feeling that His prophecy would soon be fulfilled. Who could say whether another week would find Him still among us? The thought of Him being as close as Simon's house without being able to see Him was almost more than I could bear.

The night of the party I sat home alone. Conversation and laughter floated upon the evening breeze, and I knew Jesus was near. How I longed to be in His presence! How I wanted to thank Him again for the change He'd wrought in my life! I wept and prayed for one last opportunity to be near Him. And then an idea began forming in my mind.

I had in my hope chest an alabaster box of spikenard that I had purchased at great cost some years before. At the time I bought it I was trying to fill a void in my life with possessions, which were the only things that gave me any sense of self-worth. Jesus had more than filled that empty space, though, and now I was overflowing with gratitude. I determined to attend the feast uninvited and there to anoint His feet.

Quickly I found the box of spikenard and hurried out into the night. As I passed along the streets of Bethany I formed my plan. I would enter the back door of Simon's house and go through the kitchen into the banqueting room. It would be dimly lit, and if I stayed low, I could pass behind the guests without being seen. I would find Jesus at the head of the table, quietly anoint His feet, and then slip out unnoticed by anyone except Him.

Everything went as planned, until I opened the perfume. In my haste to do something for Jesus, I had forgotten how overpowering spikenard can be. Conversation came to a sudden halt as the fragrance instantly filled the room. Concealment was impossible, and I was the focus of attention.

I became flustered and self-conscious. My ears burned, and my hands felt heavy. In my embarrassment, I awkwardly dropped the alabaster box, spilling its contents all over Jesus' feet. I didn't know what to do. I hadn't thought to bring a towel, and I had nothing with which to clean up the mess. Though only a woman of the street would ever be seen in public with her hair down, I could think of nothing else to use, so I pulled the pins from my tresses and began blotting up the spill with my hair. I also began to weep, and I'm sure I must have been a sight.

In the stillness I heard someone say, "Why this great waste? This perfume could have been sold and the money given to the poor!"

I realized that was true, and I wished it was what I had done. I remember thinking, *Jesus probably wishes the same.* And then I felt His hand upon my head.

"It's all right," He said. "She has done a good thing."

I looked up into His eyes, and He smiled at me. I knew then that I would not trade being at His feet for anything else in this world!

Grief and Gladness

One week later I was at His feet once more, only this time it was very different. Thursday night He was taken captive by the leaders of our nation, and by Friday morning He had been sentenced to death.

That morning I had come into Jerusalem from Bethany for the Passover. As I neared the city I heard the roar of a mob and followed the noise to Pilate's judgment hall. I could not believe what I saw there!

Jesus had been stripped of His clothes and beaten so badly that at first I did not recognize Him. Flogged flesh hung loosely from His back and sides. A crown of thorns had been pressed upon His head. His eyes were almost swollen shut, and His lips had been split by blows. Through the blood on His face I could see ugly bruises. He looked so battered that I could not bear the scene and hid my face from Him.

The next time I looked, they had placed a murderer beside Him, and Pilate was asking the crowd to choose which one he should set free. To my amazement, the crowd called for the release of Barabbas! Pilate could not believe their reaction either, and he motioned for silence.

"What shall be done with Jesus of Nazareth?" he asked.

"Let Him be crucified!" roared the mob.

With all that was in me, I cried out for His release. *Free Him! He is innocent!* I was struck in the face and spat upon by the rabble surrounding me, but I only cried louder.

It was clear that the crowd would be satisfied with nothing less than His death. For a time Pilate hesitated, but in the end He gave in to their wishes, saying, "Take Him, then, and crucify Him, but know that I find Him innocent!"

I followed the crowd, weeping as He carried His cross to Golgotha. The soldiers did their bloody work, and from the crowd I watched Him there. He was high and lifted up, and from His feet fell great drops of blood. I managed to press and squeeze my way through the crowd until at last I came to the foot of the cross.

His breath came in hoarse gulps as He fought to maintain consciousness, but He saw me there. I know He did! Though He said nothing, His eyes flickered in recognition, and I determined to stay near Him to the end.

The hours passed, and I lost all sense of time. An unnatural darkness came over us, and a cloud enveloped the cross. I heard Him pray for forgiveness for the mob that crucified Him. I heard Him express thirst. I heard Him calling out for His Father, but only thunder replied.

In the lightning's flash I saw His chest heaving, and then I heard Him cry in a voice that seemed to encompass the earth, "It is *finished!* Father, into Your hands I commit My spirit."

For a moment His face shone like the sun, then His head fell to His chest, and an empty silence overtook us there. I longed to remove His body, to hide it from the gaping crowd, but I could do nothing. So I stood in tears at His feet.

Eventually two men came with burial supplies and lowered His body from the cross. They wrapped it in a sheet, and I followed at a distance as they carried Him to a tomb. I saw where they placed Him. I watched them roll the stone across the entrance. For a long time I sat beside that tomb, then in grief I stumbled the empty miles to Bethany and home.

At His Feet Once More

Sabbath came and went. I slept little and moved as if in a dream. I kept hoping I would waken to find the nightmare over. I remember walking numbly to the edge of town and sitting beside the empty tomb where Lazarus had been buried. There I recalled that Jesus had said, "I am the resurrection and the life."

He had given life to others. How could it be that His own could be taken? When Lazarus came forth, I had thought that death had met its match. Now the grave had taken Him who said that He was the way, the truth, and the life. Death was victorious after all, and even the best of men could not prevent its sting. Such were my thoughts as the hours dragged painfully by.

Out of exhaustion I finally slept a few hours during the second night after Jesus' death. Sometime after midnight I awoke with the overwhelming desire to return to the tomb where Jesus was. I knew that the tomb was sealed and that a Roman guard had been posted. I knew that it would be impossible to see His body, but I just wanted to be near Him. I had always known comfort in His presence before; perhaps the same could still be mine even now. And so in tears I walked the two or three miles to Jerusalem.

Along the way I met Joanna, Salome, and Mary the mother of James taking more spices to the tomb. I joined them, and we continued walking together. About a mile from the grave we were suddenly thrown with violence to the ground. The earth heaved and shook, and a sound like thunder filled my ears. In the distance I could hear the clatter of rocks tumbling down a hillside, and my heart became fearful. Was this death's way of boasting, or was all creation groaning without Jesus?

The tremors subsided, and cautiously we rose to our feet. We continued toward the tomb, wondering whether the quake had disturbed His body or affected the hillside that contained His grave. It had! The guards had fled, but how I wished they had stayed, for the sepulchre was rent, and Jesus' body had been taken.

My grief knew no bounds! Not only was Jesus dead, but they had taken away His body, and I did not know where they had taken Him. Being robbed of His body was more injustice than I could bear. In despair I turned and ran to tell the disciples.

When Peter and John heard the news, they raced to the tomb, and I followed some distance behind. By the time I got there, they had gone, and I was alone. I went to the entrance of the tomb and looked inside.

Through my tears I saw two men sitting where the body of Jesus had lain. One of them asked why I was crying, and I told him that I had wanted to be near Jesus but that someone had taken His body and I didn't know where it was. I didn't feel like talking more, so I turned away, and when I did I saw Someone standing in my path. It was another Man, and He too asked me why I was weeping.

At His question I fell further apart and began sobbing uncontrollably. I tried to talk, but could only moan. I struggled to gain composure, but it would not come. I thought He was the gardener, and brokenly I tried to ask if He knew where they had taken my Lord.

Perhaps Joseph's sepulchre was considered too fine for a carpenter. If that was the case, I knew of another empty tomb just outside Bethany. I could take Him there if they would let me. Through my tears I told Him so.

And then I heard Him speak my name. "Mary," He said, and my heart stood still. "Mary!" It was Jesus!

I fell at His feet and cried, "Master!"

He told me not to touch Him yet, and then He gave me a message for His friends. He said that He was going to the Father and that everything was going to be all right. I'd heard Him talk about "going" before. At *that* time He had said He would come again and receive us to Himself. He said we would be able to be with Him there, and now that is what I live for.

One day He will do for others what He did for our family and for Lazarus. He will come to waken His friends from their long sleep. I expect to hear Him call my name again then. I understand that He plans to give us each a crown, and I can hardly wait to cast mine at His feet!

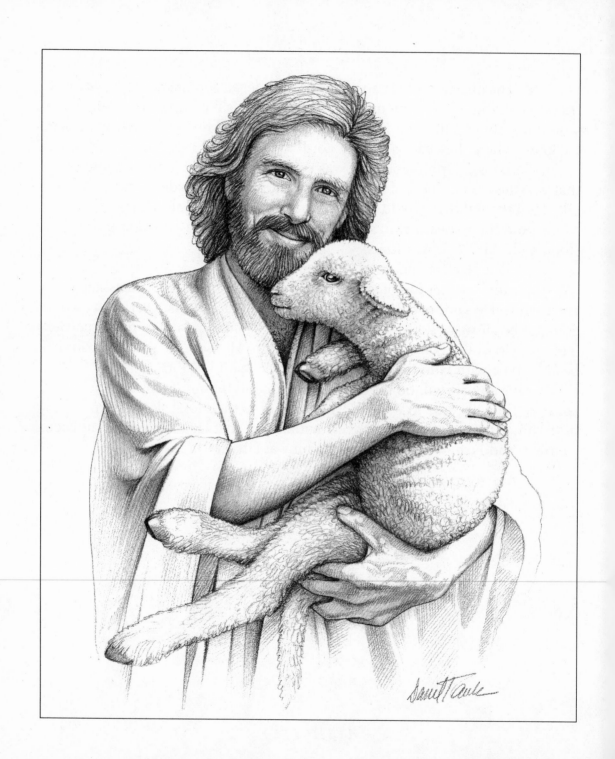

CHAPTER NINE

Hand Out

I was with my father the first time I saw Him. I was 14 years old, and father had begun taking me into the fields with him to watch the flock. I'm a shepherd by inheritance, you see. Where we lived in Bethlehem, sheep were quite valuable for their wool. Our sheep, however, were bred and raised for another purpose.

Our flock was Passover stock. We bred sheep to produce unblemished lambs that were sold for Pesach sacrifice each year. During Passover in Jerusalem, an unblemished lamb brought a price five or six times its normal market value. Why, a shepherd with good stock could earn nearly his entire annual income in a week!

So it was for good reason that I was a shepherd-in-training the night the angels sang. With other shepherds, we were gathered around the communal fire as we talked about a puzzling verse in one of the prophecies of Isaias. It was a verse that says the Messiah would be led like a lamb to the slaughter. It seemed inconceivable to us that the Messiah would die like one of our Passover sheep—and for what purpose?

All at once the plain was lighted by an unearthly light, which caused our bonfire to dim by comparison. Though our *flocks* seemed unaware of it, we were startled with fear and tried to shield our faces from the glory. We heard a voice before we saw the form of the angel. His words calmed our hearts and thrilled our souls, for he said, "Don't be afraid! I have good news for you and people everywhere! This day, for you, in the city of David, the Saviour has been born!"

And suddenly with this angel there was a multitude of others like him, singing the most beautiful music ever heard by human ears. They sang about glory and God and peace for men, whom He loves. And they told us another thing even more wonderful: they told us that *we could find* this Saviour in a simple manger just outside of town.

Nobody in town seemed to know anything about the birth of a baby, and some time passed before we came upon the manger where He lay. At first His father wasn't going to let us in, but when we told of the angels' visit and song, he gave us welcome and motioned for us to enter the stable. An olive oil lamp was the only light in the place, but by its flickering we saw the Child.

When the angel said that the Baby had been laid in a manger, I thought it a strange place for the Messiah. The stable *was* plain, as were the garments of His parents. The Babe was wrapped in an old blanket, and there were farm animals about. He was alert, wide-eyed, and blinking. His little hands jerked and grasped spasmodically, the way infants do. In one hand He clutched a long piece of straw, but as I gazed through the half-light and shadows of that place, somehow the straw appeared to me as a scepter and the manger became the throne room of a king. Overcome, I knelt and worshiped Him there.

The memory of that night and those tiny hands has stayed with me for more than 30 years now. I've come to understand that those hands in the stable were the reaching hands of God. But let me tell you more about them so that you might understand as well.

A few months after that wonderful night our family got word that my father's parents in Nazareth were ailing. We moved our flocks and family to that town to be with them in their final years. That is where I saw the Child again.

Shortly after King Herod died, I was with our flock near the edge of town, beside the road that led toward Egypt. A young couple with a small boy approached along the road, and at first I gave them little notice. As they drew nearer, however, I felt as though I had seen them before. I cast about in my memory for when and where it might have been. Suddenly I knew! The place had been a stable at night! These two travelers had been beside a manger-crib, and this small Boy had been a king. Like a man in a dream, I slowly lifted my hand in a sort of waving salute. The Child waved back.

Well, the couple took up housekeeping in Nazareth, and soon the man had opened a modest carpentry shop. As the months and years went by, I watched the Child's growth with keen interest. During His earlier years His mother would often bring Him out to the fields and meadows at the edge of town, and they would have picnics. Many times while grazing my flock I would watch from a distance as He brought flowers to His mother, climbed trees, threw rocks, and engaged in the wonderful occupations of a child. *Life* seemed to overflow with exuberance for this Boy.

Once in springtime He timidly approached me with a request to pet one of the lambs. He was particularly attracted to a smaller one that had been born with a lame foreleg. He scooped the pitiful little thing into His arms, where it returned His affection by nuzzling His neck. Because of its deformity, I knew that the lamb would never go to market, so I asked the Boy if He would like to take it home as a pet. When His mother gave permission, He clapped His hands with joy and gave the lamb such a hug that I jokingly cautioned Him against strangling the little creature. He laughed at my joke, but I heard Him whisper to the lamb, "At least you won't have to die on an altar."

As the years passed, the Child grew as much in kindness as in stature. It was a common thing in Nazareth to see Him on some mission of mercy. He would bring His supper for a beggar to devour or share His lunch with a stray and hungry dog. If ever He saw other children abusing an animal, He would come to its aid; more than once I saw rocks meant for a dog deflected by His body. On occasion in springtime He could be seen returning a baby bird to its nest. He had a particular interest in lost creatures and loved to help shepherds search for a missing sheep. He would carry water for ladies in our town, seemingly unconcerned that it was "women's work." Once I even saw Him carry a waterpot for a Roman girl whom the neighborhood children had been cruelly teasing.

In their carpentry shop He was a great help to His father as well. Farmers stood in line for the yokes His hands had made. He was so careful in shaping and smoothing the wood that a yoke of oxen seemed hardly to notice the weight of the burdens they bore. He worked long and hard for His father, but always in the morning and often at twilight I would see Him climbing the hills above town, where He would lift His eyes and hands toward heaven.

He was praying there, and sometimes I had the good fortune to be near enough so that His voice came across the slopes to my ears. Such prayers they were! Why, He would talk to God like you or I would talk to our father. He would go over plans, talk about the day, or make requests that were quite unlike those made by the scribes or Pharisees.

The cycles of life and seasons continued with regularity, and then one day He left our town. Most of what He did during the three or so years that followed came to me on the lips of travelers, and each new story filled my heart with wonder.

I've heard that the hands I had seen in a stable helped pull on the oars and nets of a Galilean fishing boat to bring in a record catch.

I've heard that He would touch the bent legs of a cripple and in touching make them well. The diseased flesh of lepers, deemed untouchable, He would touch, and a wonderful thing would happen to them. It was said that if He touched the eyes of the blind, they would see. Sickness and disease fled like night before sunrise at the touch of His hand. If ever He knocked on the door of a home where pain resided, those who lived there were sure to be surprised by joy! Once He touched the funeral bier of a widow's child, and another time He took the cold hand of a sleeping maid in His. In both cases, though they were dead, yet did they live!

Though it was reported that He raised a whip in the Temple and overthrew the money changers' tables, still the same hands spread in blessing shortly after, and children of the poor climbed upon His lap to feel a gentler touch. He especially loved the little children and would often hold them or pat the head of one who drew near Him in a crowd.

I've heard that with those hands He broke bread and fish enough to feed thousands. With those hands He lifted a fisherman named Peter from a watery grave and a woman named Mary from a living death. With *one* hand He pulled a cripple to his feet near the pool of Bethesda. With *one* hand He sent terror-stricken demons into the waters of Galilee.

I wish that all I had to tell was as wonderful, but one Thursday evening, in an attic room after washing the feet of some friends, He foretold events that shame me to retell. In His hands He held broken pieces of bread that He said were as His body soon would be. He held and drank from a cup containing wine as nearly red as His blood that soon would flow. And He made a promise then not to drink of the fruit of the vine again until He would drink it new with us in His Father's kingdom.

Afterward they exchanged that upper room for a garden, where His hands clutched at clumps of grass and soil as He pleaded for another way. He was not given one, but an angel came to cradle His head and strengthen His hands to take the bitter cup.

Then came a wicked mob that bound His hands by torchlight, but not tight enough to prevent them reaching out to restore the severed ear of an enemy. They remained tied after that, however, as He was led and shoved from one farce of a trial to another. He did not lift them to protect Himself from the lash, the club, or the spittle of brutish men. They did to Him what they would, but like the lambs I sold for sacrifice, He uttered not a word.

Though bleeding from wounds in His head and upper body, He still courageously lifted the rough-hewn timbers of a heavy cross whose splinters pierced His hands. After dragging it only a short distance, He stumbled in exhaustion upon hard cobblestones, but He struggled to rise again after wiping the blood from His eyes.

I had come to Jerusalem because of Passover and to sell my lambs. We were grazing a flock on a hill overlooking the city when the size and roar of a crowd near the western gate attracted my attention. Intending to find out the reason for such commotion, I left the flock with my herdsman and reached the crowd's edge just in time to see Roman soldiers nail Him to the cross. His hands jerked and twitched spasmodically, and suddenly I recalled an infant's hand by lamplight the night the angels sang.

Where are they now? I wondered. He did too, for with a voice that seemed to ring across creation, He cried, "My God, My God! Why have You forsaken Me?" An earthquake was His only answer, then silence and a distant moaning wind.

Sympathizers lowered Him from the cross and folded His hands in death upon His chest. He was buried in a borrowed tomb, but did not stay there long! Two days later, as the sun rose, with His own hands He folded the grave clothes and stepped out into glory.

The scars remain, however, because two in Emmaus saw His hands as He blessed their food. He still employs those hands in deeds of kindness, for I am told that one morning shortly thereafter He prepared a fire and breakfast for some friends at the lake.

He left us from a mountaintop, and I was among those who saw Him go. He said, "I am with you always, even to the end of the world." Then He lifted His hands in blessing and began to rise as though some unearthly power was attracting Him to a better place. Just before He was lost in a cloud, like a man in a dream, I slowly lifted my hand in a sort of waving salute. He waved back. I thought I saw seven stars in His hand, but it may have only been reflected light.

I raise sheep for wool now. Sacrifices are not needed anymore. Before He left He said that He was going to the Father, His *and ours.* Stephen said that he saw Him standing at the right hand of God, but it seems to me that He *is* the right hand of God, and I'm thankful that He lived and moved for a time among us!

CHAPTER TEN

Talítha Cumí

My name is Jairus. I live in Capernaum, and I love two women. That's all right, however, because one is my wife, Deborah, and the other is my 12-year-old daughter. Though her name is actually Diana, I affectionately call her Princess, and she knows why. She's more precious than a king's daughter to me, and were I a king, I would give the whole of my kingdom in exchange for her life if it became necessary.

Actually, I *am* a ruler, not of a kingdom, but of a synagogue, and there was a time when my position made things very difficult for me. The difficulty mainly involved two people, Princess and a Man named Jesus of Nazareth. Let me tell you more about each of them.

Princess brightens our home with her laughter and singing. She has always been a cheerful child. Her frequent smiles, so full of happiness, have a way of spilling over onto whomever she is near, and her zest for living is contagious. That is why for Deborah and me it was as if the sun had ceased to shine when our daughter became deathly sick. But I'm getting ahead of myself.

You need to know about Jesus. In my country our economy centers on the Temple and the sacrificial system. Those who are most influential are the priests and religious rulers. They sit on the seat of wealth and power. The people have always followed their leaders religiously—and to a great extent mindlessly—until this young Carpenter from Nazareth came along.

He talks about a *friendly* Father God who accepts sinners with open arms. He teaches that God is more interested in mercy than in sacrifice. He attacks our religious traditions, calls the leaders hypocrites and snakes, and claims that the ground is level when humans stand before God. He says God has no grandchildren, only sons and daughters, and that *anyone* can be His child.

Speaking of children, Jesus talks and plays with them as readily as He talks to adults. He tells stories and uses such simple language that thinking people sometimes feel insulted. "Scandalous" is the word the leaders use in describing His teachings. Religion is big business in Israel, and quite frankly, Jesus was bad for business.

He especially affected my business because He spent a lot of His time in and around Capernaum. He is here so often that the people have begun to call it "His city." Attendance has been down for synagogue services, and I tend to agree with my friends in Jerusalem who say, "The whole world has gone after Him."

Even my wife and daughter went after Him for a time. Once, they came back from a lakeshore gathering where He spoke and told me that a huge crowd had listened spellbound through lunch and all afternoon to the things He said. Princess enthusiastically told me that Jesus healed the lame, the sick, and even a leper. They told me I should come and see Him for myself. I told them no synagogue ruler would be caught listening to the teachings of a *carpenter,* and I forbade them, as my family, to ever again go where He was.

Then my Princess became ill. One day she was playing, laughing, and singing; the next she was bedridden and in terrible pain. Her forehead burned with fever, and she complained of severe stomach cramps. Nothing she ate or drank would stay down. In fact, she came to the point of vomiting bile and blood.

Deborah and I were frantic! Nothing we did seemed to make any difference, and I ached to see her so very sick. We called the doctor, and the news he gave us was devastating. He told us her symptoms were identical to those of a young boy he had been called to treat the week before. I asked how the boy was now, and he didn't answer me at first. I pressed him with my question until finally he said, "His parents buried him yesterday."

I was overwhelmed with grief! I went to Princess and sat beside her bed. I bathed her brow and stroked her flaming cheeks. I kept a vigil by her side the rest of the day and all that night. She slept restlessly between bouts with pain. When she would waken, I would try to get her to take some liquid, but she refused to drink or eat. I asked her if there was *anything* I could bring her, and her answer startled me. "Yes," she said, "Jesus."

Oh, how I struggled with that request! I loved my daughter, and I would have spent all I had to see her healthy again. I would have secured any physician, bought any medicines, done anything humanly possible for her, but I couldn't ask *Him* for help.

For one thing, He was in opposition to much of what I did and taught as synagogue ruler. For another, I questioned whether He really healed anyway, suspecting rather that His "miracles" were just hocus-pocus and trickery. And a further thought troubled me. *Even if He could do something, He surely wouldn't do it for a doubter and skeptic like me. He wouldn't come to my house.*

Two more days passed, and her condition worsened. I prayed, pleading with God for her life, but I felt that my prayers got no higher than the ceiling. It seemed God was not there for me! Ruler though I was, my position wouldn't help me now.

My neighbor came over and asked if there was something he could do to help. Bitterly and with some sarcasm, I told him he could arrange for the hired mourners, because we had no hope of her recovery.

If you've never sat by the bed of a dying loved one, you'll not know how desperately helpless I felt. I held her hand tightly, as if my grasp could keep her from slipping away. Time seemed to race and drag at once. Her breathing began to rattle in her chest, and suddenly my desperation pushed me past my pride. I bolted for the door and began running down the cobble-stone street toward the edge of town.

Tears blurred my vision, and I stumbled on the rough roadway. I fell to my knees, scraping them and my hands as well, but I was numb to pain. I scrambled back to my feet and continued running recklessly toward the out-skirts of Capernaum. My breath came rapidly, my throat burned, my muscles screamed, but I couldn't stop now. I had only one thought and hope. Jesus!

I saw the crowd first, and then I saw Him. Out of deference to my position, or maybe because they saw my desperation, the crowd let me through, and the next thing I remember, I had fallen at His feet. I clutched at the hem of His garment and gasped out, "Please . . . please! My daughter is dying! I pray You, please come and touch her so that she may be healed! I can't bear for her to die!"

Quickly He bent down and, taking my hands in His, lifted me. "Let's go," He said, and we turned ourselves toward home. But the crowd slowed our progress, and I remember thinking, *I've come to Him too late!*

That was the longest mile I ever walked, and then my worst fears came true. I saw friends and neighbors coming in our direction. "She died," they said. "There's no use bringing Jesus now. It's too late."

I wished I too could die! I had let her down. She had asked me to get Jesus, but I left too late. The noise and feel of the crowd faded, and in my anguish I felt suddenly alone. Jesus *had been willing* to come to my house, but I hadn't asked Him soon enough. I seemed to be sinking into darkness, and then I felt Him take my arm and heard Him say, "Don't be afraid. Trust Me. She's going to be all right!"

I pressed closer to Jesus, and together we hurried toward my home. Before we got there we could hear the mourners I had asked for. As we approached my yard, the volume of their wailing increased. Looking in their direction, Jesus held up His right hand as if signaling a pause. The mourners hushed expectantly. Every eye was on Jesus, and every ear heard Him say, "Why do you make so much commotion and cry like that? This little girl is not dead! She is only sleeping."

For a moment there was silence. Then one of the mourners walked up to Jesus and spat at His feet. "Who are You to come here at a time like this with Your jokes? If that was meant to be funny, we are not amused!"

"Maybe in Nazareth they don't know the difference between death and sleep," said another mourner. "But in this town, we call death by its right name. There is a difference, you know, between the two! When people stop breathing, it is not because they fell asleep! We have seen her ourselves, and she is *dead!*"

By this time the wailing had changed to jeers and laughter. "Listen to me, *Carpenter*," said one of my servants. "The *physician* has pronounced her dead, and I suggest that You return to Your carpenter shop and work with wood. You obviously don't know how to work with people. You are *not* welcome here. Leave!"

Jesus looked from one face to another. His eyes arrested their laughter. Then He spoke deliberately, calmly, and quietly, though His voice seemed to rip through the crowd like thunder. *"You . . . leave,"* He said. Then motioning for three of His disciples to follow, He took my arm, moved me through the open door of my home, and shut it behind us.

Like a man in a dream, I led the way to the room where my daughter lay. Deborah was kneeling beside the bed. Her upper body lay across the still chest of our child, and her arms cradled Diana's head against her cheek. She was sobbing uncontrollably, and seeing them there loosed the fountain of my own tears. Regardless of what Jesus called it, my daughter *was dead!*

Then I looked at Jesus and realized that *He* was the one who was most saddened! His own eyes brimmed over, and His face seemed to say that a girl like that shouldn't be dead. It can't be true. She *is* only sleeping, and I will teach My enemy that he should leave children well enough alone.

Gently He helped Deborah to her feet, turning her toward me. I reached for her, and we clung to each other. Then Jesus moved toward the bed, and time stood still. He stood looking down on Diana's ashen face, and then, stooping slightly, He reached out with His right hand and gently stroked her cheek.

A silence came over all of us as we watched and wondered. I could feel my heartbeat pulsing in my neck and temples. Deborah's grip on my hand tightened. The room seemed to grow suddenly brighter, and I wondered if my emotions were playing tricks on my senses.

Jesus took Diana's hand as one would take the hand of a queen while helping her down a staircase. And then He spoke. "Princess," He said, "Princess, I say to you, arise!"

As if it was possible! And it *was!* A tremor passed through her unconscious form. Her lips unclosed in a smile, and her eyes opened widely, as if from sleep. She sat up and gave Jesus a hug, as our hearts overflowed with joy!

We now wept tears of another sort and stumbled over each other in our rush to embrace them both. Jesus smiled and moved to one side as our family was reunited. I could tell that He shared our joy, much like a grandparent might beam beside the cradle of the newest grandchild.

For a while we were so overcome with happiness that no one spoke. Then Jesus made a thoughtful suggestion. "Having not eaten for so long," He said, "she must be hungry. Why don't you give her some food?"

That made sense to Deborah, and she hurried toward the kitchen to prepare something for us all. Still clinging to Diana, I turned toward Jesus and said, "Master, it is impossible for me to thank You or tell You how grateful I am for what You have done! Were I to outlive Methuselah, I would still sing Your praises till the day I die."

I will always wonder about His reply. "Please don't tell anyone what has happened here today."

I would like to be able to honor His request, but let me ask *you*, "Could *you* keep quiet about what He has done?"

CHAPTER 11

Sonset on Nazareth

My Son was returning. It had been almost three years since He was last home, and His closest friends have told me that He has a longing to once more walk the dusty paths and winding ways of His childhood and youth. Some might call it homesickness—and they would be partially right—but I know this longing speaks of more than homesickness.

You see, for the past several years He has spent His days and nights as a sort of migrant. Never really knowing where He will next lay His head, He has moved from village to village, town to town. Friends or companions? For the most part they come and go, depending upon the sway of popular opinion. One day I hear that the people wish to make Him king; the next day I hear that they drove Him from their town.

In the surrounding areas the people know Him by many names. Teacher, Rabboni, the Nazarene, the Rabble-rouser, and among others, the *Miracle Worker*. I know when He hears that name He understands that He is usually sought because of His power. Seldom do people talk of His love and compassion, but He would rather be sought because of Himself. After all, His entire purpose revolves around touching people on a heart-to-heart level, giving of Himself. Yet the usual action of those who seek Him is to bypass the Man, desiring only His power, His gifts. For Him, that is a real disappointment, a heartfelt grief, a lonely sorrow.

It seems to me that He is merely being used, but there is something that hurts Him more deeply than that knowledge. The real pain comes because He wishes to be more than a "wonder worker." His deepest desire has always been to be a friend, but one-way friendship is a lonely place. He wants to give *Himself* and not merely His power. I have often wondered why the people make it so hard for Him to give Himself. Why are so few willing to become His friend? Why do the crowds disperse when their sick have been restored? Why must He always walk alone?

I was watching from the window when He entered our village. This is where He grew up, and I prayed, "Oh, God, let Him find what He came back for. Perhaps the friends He longs for will be found among those with whom He has lived and worked through the years."

As I watched I saw Thamar, our village grocer, step out of his shop, and I heard my Son call out, "Hello, Thamar! It sure is *good* to see you again!"

I could scarcely believe the grocer's reply as he said, "Well if it isn't the Happy Wanderer. What brings You to our town? I thought You were too good to walk these streets."

There was sorrow in His voice as my Son answered, "Too good to walk the streets of My hometown? Why, Thamar, I was really looking forward . . ."

Then it seemed my heart felt the prick of a sword as my stepson Joses sneeringly called out from across the street, "Hometown is it? If this is Your hometown, then why are we the last to receive Your privileged attention?"

A crowd began forming as people recognized Him and pointed Him out to others. "Hey, isn't He called the miracle worker?" shouted a man in the crowd.

"No," answered another voice, "His title is prophet."

"I thought He was a doctor," laughed another in the crowd. "I've *heard* that He heals the sick."

Then my own neighbor lady called out, "Don't you believe it. He lived next door to me for almost 30 years, and I never saw Him heal a soul."

Standing in the center of this commotion, my Son slowly turned His gaze from one face to another. The haughty crowd had formed a circle around Him, and I knew that He suddenly felt intensely alone. This was His *home-town*. The village where He grew up, where He had worked side by side with many of those who were now jeering.

My heart ached for Him as the catcalls and hooting continued. As someone said, "Hey, Magician, let's see You do some of Your tricks here," I wondered why they hated Him.

Another voice loudly asserted, "I bet He can't even cure the common cold!"

How could they be so cruel? His greatest desire was to be their friend. Why, then, did they resist Him so? Why did they make it so hard for Him to do that?

One of the villagers offered a challenge, saying, "Come on, Prophet, aren't You at least going to defend Yourself? Don't You have anything to say?"

I felt the sword prick more deeply as I watched Him there. He said nothing in reply, but looked from one heckler to another. Something in His eyes reminded me of sheep I've seen being led to slaughter.

My own heart was so heavy that I was about to turn away, when I noticed Him seem to become oblivious to the jostling, jeering crowd. His attention had been drawn toward the hunched figure of an elderly man sitting with His back against a nearby well. The noise of the surrounding throng faded to dim confusion as in my mind's eye I recalled days gone by.

The lonely, hunched figure was that of Shemaiah. Old Shemaiah, His friend, blind from birth. The people of Nazareth were accustomed to the stooped and groping figure of this blind man who had no family or friends. He was usually ignored about town, since most in the sighted world were too busy to befriend an old blind man.

But I remembered times when I had seen Jesus as a child watching the neighborhood children softly laughing and pointing as the blind man stumbled over sticks they would place in his path. I remember Him telling me that the townspeople would mimic the man's sightless, shuffling walk, and that they would give wide berth when the blind man lay groping on the ground, trying to find his cane after having tripped over an unnoticed stone.

From this same window I had seen my Son rush to the aid of blind Shemaiah, and together they would walk from place to place. They could often be seen traveling together, the sightless one and my Boy. Jesus was the blind man's eyes, and as the years passed, they would spend long afternoons walking side by side in the fields and paths. Jesus told me that Shemaiah would listen gratefully as He would describe the lovely scenes of nature. And I was glad for the deep bond of friendship that developed between them.

Now as Jesus gazed at the solitary figure beside the well, I knew He was remembering the companionship that Shemaiah had provided, the understanding. Shemaiah had accepted Him for *Himself,* and many times I remember Jesus telling me how He wished there were something we could do to restore the blind man's sight.

The crowd became hushed. As all eyes followed Jesus' gaze, they too saw the stooped figure with vacant stare. Many in that crowd could also recall with vivid memory when a young Boy and a blind man had walked arm in arm through the fields and paths of Nazareth.

Suddenly a harsh voice broke the silence. "Bring old Shemaiah over here," it said. "Someone go and get the blind one. We'll see a miracle one way or another."

"Splendid idea," echoed another voice. "This prophet will surely heal His old friend."

"Yes," laughed my neighbor, "if He really *is* a miracle worker, He won't pass up a chance to do something for no-eyes over there."

Two men from the crowd brought Shemaiah over and shoved Him toward Jesus. As the crowd laughed, the blind man stumbled forward, but found himself caught, supported by two familiar arms. I saw him grasp Jesus' broad shoulders and falteringly pull himself to his feet. His wrinkled hands traced the features of Jesus' face, and I knew as his fingers lightly crossed my Son's cheeks that he would feel a warm moistness trickling from those compassionate eyes.

Then Jesus lifted His arms and grasped one of the blind man's wrists with each of His own strong, firm hands. Gently pressing the old one's wrinkled hands against His cheeks, He leaned forward and looked with pity into Shemaiah's sightless eyes. He *still* longed to give sight to those eyes! I knew what He wanted to do for this man whom the crowd was jeering. I saw His chin tremble, and straining my ears, I heard Him say, "Shemaiah! Oh, My *friend,* Shemaiah."

A smile brightened the face of the sightless one, and with appreciative voice he answered, "Jesus!" (He was the only villager to call Him by that name.) "Jesus, how good of You to remember blind old Shemaiah. You didn't forget me, Jesus!"

In an instant I heard Jesus answer, "I will *never* forget you, Shemaiah. You're one of My friends."

Then He looked at the watching throng and hesitated a moment, with a wistful look in His eyes. I caught my breath, wondering if perhaps He was going to give sight to His blind friend. Then slowly He moved toward the outskirts of town. The crowd parted, making way as He passed.

I heard someone from the back of the crowd shout, "What's wrong, Miracle Worker? Did You forget how to do Your healing-the-blind trick?"

He turned toward the questioning voice and paused. There was a look of deep pain upon His face. After a moment's thought, He replied with a disappointed voice that betrayed the sorrow I knew was within, "Truly a prophet is without honor in His hometown."

"Of all the nerve!" shouted Joses. "Did you hear what He said? He thinks He's a prophet."

"The sacrilege of such words!" cried another. "He ought to be stoned." "Yes, stone Him," echoed a dozen angry voices. "That's what we should do. Stone Him. Stone Him! *Stone Him!*"

The crowd was in an uproar now, and several men began throwing rocks at Jesus' back as He slowly walked away. A large jagged rock landed forcefully between His shoulder blades, and the impact caused Him to lurch forward onto His knees. I wanted to run to Him then and throw my arms around Him and tell the crowd to go away, but I watched helplessly from my window as He struggled to His feet and continued walking away, without looking back at the jeering, laughing crowd.

Once the object of their ridicule was no longer available to direct their curses toward, the crowd dispersed. One by one they drifted back to homes or jobs. I could hear them jesting about the "Miracle Worker" and complimenting one another that they had "not been taken in by such a trickster, such a deceiver."

At last the streets were quiet again, empty except for the lone figure of a blind man who once more sat with his back against the well. The vacant stare was still present, but now I noticed that there was a smile upon his wrinkled face. He was talking to himself, and I caught the words "Jesus, Jesus, why does everyone reject Him? They cursed and swore at Him, yet He answered them not a word. How could anyone keep quiet through all that? He is more than a man. I have heard Him called Messiah, God's Son. If ever anyone was God's Son, it would be Him. . . ."

Then I saw what Shemaiah, wrapped in thought, was unaware of. Jesus was returning down the deserted street! Suddenly Shemaiah became aware that something was blocking the sunlight that had been warming his sky-turned face. The late-afternoon sun caused a lengthened and distorted shadow to fall from the figure who stood before the blind man. From within the shadow a hand moved out into the sunlight. Fingers gently touched first one and then the other eye of the blind man's upturned face. The hand was drawn back, and the shadow disappeared as Jesus walked toward home.

I met Him at the door, and we embraced. "I'm sorry," I said. "They were mean to You."

"It's all right," my Boy answered. "We got to help Shemaiah, didn't we?" And then He was gone.

I looked back out the window at Shemaiah, who remained seated with his back still against the stone wall of the well. The smile was still on his lips, but a change was visible. The vacant stare was conspicuously absent, and I thought how glad I was that Jesus was his friend!

I turned my attention from Shemaiah to the narrow path that ascended the mountain above our town. Far above Nazareth I could see a solitary figure making His way toward the mountain pass. The sun's rays gave His shadow a lengthy and distorted form. Towering white clouds were scattered across the stretching sky. I saw Him draw His coat tightly about His neck and shoulders as He leaned into the wind and continued walking.

Just below the pass He paused and, turning, looked back toward our valley. His face was only an outline, but I'm sure there was a broad smile upon it. I saw Him look up into the endless blue heavens, and I know Him well enough to tell you that He was whispering, "Thank You, Father." He continued walking then, but just before He crossed the skyline, He turned and waved.

And in a small town where the mountain meets the plain, a mother's heartache was lifted, and an old man gazed in rapture at his first sunset.

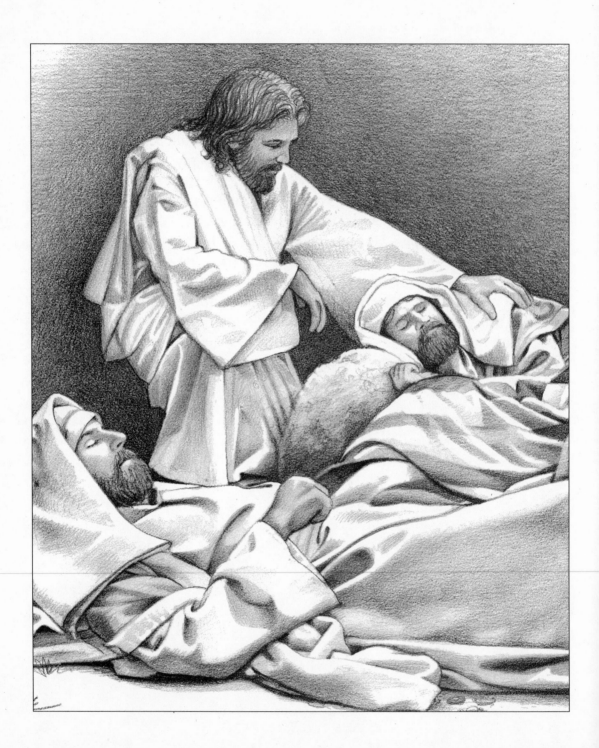

CHAPTER 12

The Night Was April

You have heard and considered the fast of 40 days that the Man from Nazareth endured? There was yet another fast, more intense in its severity, more painful in its sufferings. This fast also was undertaken willingly. The details are scarce, for He endured it alone. And no one but Him was aware of its awful significance.

The night is April. Pale spring mists creep silently through the branches of trees standing dark against a cloud-patched sky. A brook tumbles musically down the mountainside. The wind moans faintly from some higher slope. Cloud-scattered moonlight brightens the shadowy places, now and then revealing a small group of sleeping men who seem unmindful of the cold and damp. A dark Figure approaches noiselessly. Moving through the trees on bare feet, He pauses in a shadow, observing each member of the sleeping group.

They sleep, for it is late—the darkest hour of night. But the shadowed Watcher has not slept. With agonizing premonition, He has kept a lonely vigil. He takes no notice of the dew falling heavily upon His garments. It is His last mortal night on earth.

For a long while He has lain upon the ground, facing the sky, searching between clouds, from star to distant star. He has prayed and hoped, struggled and dreamed a wakeful dream of friends with whom to share this last night. With more than sorrow, He turns away and leaves behind the indifferent sleepers.

A cloud obscures the moon, creating a sudden heavy darkness— oppressing gloom. Stumbling, He falls heavily to the ground. Several sleepers stir groggily and peer wide-eyed into the darkness. But all is quiet once again, save for the nearby brook and distant moaning wind. One by one, shrugging in bewilderment, they return to drowsy slumber, dreaming of warmth and shelter and loved ones far away.

With labored breathing, the Man clutches at a nearby rock and pulls Himself to His knees. He tries to rise, but cannot. Again He tries, but with similar result, having grown so weak in His struggle to live. Collapsing exhausted upon the rock, He whispers, "Father, oh, Father! Is there no other way? Will no one give Me courage? Will no one give Me strength to see another sunrise?"

He moans and cradles His head in trembling hands. How He craves companionship! Summoning His reserve of waning strength, He staggers to His feet and gropes His way through the darkness, from tree to dew-draped tree. His heavy heart is wrung with a crushing, lonely sorrow. He *must* have someone to talk with, someone who will listen.

He stumbles into their clearing and gently nudges one of the slumbering figures. "James," He whispers, "James, could I talk with you awhile?" A mumble is the only answer as James shifts to a more comfortable position and resumes dreaming.

Moving on hands and knees, He tries waking another. "Peter, Peter? Can you hear Me, Peter?" But the fisherman is dead to all distraction, so the sleepless One moves on.

A little apart and to one side He finds the small-boned form of John. Somehow He is confident that John will provide the companionship He seeks. "John?" and again a whispered, "John?"

John rouses with the question "What is it, Master?"

"It's just that I feel so alone, John. I need someone to talk to. You don't have to reply, John, but listen . . . please? It's enough to know that you're there.

"Some believe a person could not ask for a better friend than himself, but it would seem to Me that they have known little sorrow, John. One who suffers places a higher value on friendship. John? John?" He too has yielded to heavy slumber.

The Master stands, sways unsteadily for a moment, then slowly moves away, casting a backward glance in the direction of His sleeping friends. Coming to the stump of a fallen tree, He sits down. Absorbed by a sense of awful helplessness, He gazes up through the space the tree had once occupied. Moon and stars, like His sleeping friends, have disappeared in darkness. Thickening clouds go scuttling before an increasing wind. The heavens seem shut from view.

With nowhere to turn and no one to talk to, He leans forward, hunching over knees, and buries His head in His hands. Wind tosses His hair and buffets His weary body. An internal counterpart to this blowing, screaming wind seems to be whirling within His brain. He massages His forehead and temples with rough and calloused hands. The sleeves of His loose-fitting garment drop away, exposing muscular forearms.

Rising suddenly to His feet, He stands squinting into the wind and at the cloud-laden sky. Eyes searching from horizon to dark horizon, He whispers as to no one, "I can't go through with this. Could these men go on without Me? Here, while eternity hangs in the balance, they sleep. There's so much yet to do, and I am young. So many sick, so many lonely, so many needing encouragement and hope! They sleep! I'm sure they want to watch with Me, but they are just too tired. I'm alone. Now, with everything at stake, there is none with Me."

The mental anguish is too much. He sways forward, off balance, and clutches at a small sapling growing within reach. His grip tightens as if clinging to life itself. His nails dig deeply into the soft outer bark. Shoulders hunched and trembling, He falteringly, tearfully pleads, "Father, please help Me! Oh, My Father, I don't think I can go on. It's so dark and cold!" His grip relaxes, and He falls heavily, helplessly forward, facedown upon the cold, damp ground. Still He somehow finds strength to form the dying words, "Nevertheless, not My will but Your will be done." At last, chest heaving with labored breath, He sleeps the fainting sleep of unconsciousness.

It is more than a loving Father can bare. The wind abruptly stills. Only drifting leaves remain to hint of the storm that was. The clouds disappear as quickly as vaporized breath on a winter's morn. The tumbling brook makes the only sound.

In the stillness of this quiet hour there appears beside the unconscious Form a being of light and glory—overcome by emotion. Stooping, he gently lifts the limp body and softly says, "Jesus? Jesus? I'm here to listen. I'm here to comfort and encourage. I'm here, Jesus, and I love You! But more than that, Your Father does too, and He sends His love!"

Eleven men still sleep. A figure approaches noiselessly on bare feet and moves among them. Standing straight and tall, He gazes tenderly down, as a father would upon His sleeping children. "Sleep on now, Simon; sleep on now, James; and you too, John. Take your rest, My friends, for there is One who watches and never sleeps!"

Tomorrow He will die, but just now He is rested and at peace. Sitting amid His circle of sleeping companions, He looks down with a lingering smile at each one, recalling memories of countless talks around the fire, the long and dusty miles, the storms weathered, rivers crossed, boating and fishing trips, their loyalty through persecution, the mutual trust and companionship. Comrades of time and experience! "The times we have shared together," He whispers, "are only beginning."

There comes a muffled sound of angry voices. He's brought abruptly from His reverie. Rising to His feet, He looks once more at these sleeping men whom He loves so much. Stooping over first one then another, He rouses them from slumber, saying, "Rise up, let us go. Lo, he who betrays Me is at hand."

CHAPTER 13

Only a Little Sin

B ut, Sir," said man, "it was only a little sin." Clang came the sound of metal hitting metal as he said it again: "Only a little sin. You know, I was wondering what would be necessary were it a sin of greater magnitude."

"The same sacrifice would be required," said the voice of Him crucified.

Again the metallic crash!

"But, Sir," questioned man, "why such intense suffering for so little wrong?"

The reply came through tightly clenched teeth and laborious breathing, "Is any wrong small?"

"I cannot answer, for I am not certain that an adequate definition of wrong can be established," bantered man, stepping aside to avoid the falling flecks of blood.

In a faltering whisper the Crucified answered, "Wrong is anything that is opposed to truth."

"Ah," said man, "but what is truth?"

Between gasping breaths for air came a hoarse reply, "I AM!"

"Huh?" responded man, turning to leave. "Look where it got You. Crucified! And for what? All this suffering for what?" And man, shrugging, turned his back to depart.

In a voice barely audible, the Crucified pleaded, as tears mingled with the blood, "For you, man! To make eternity possible for you, I AM!"

A flash of lightning. A rumbling and roar of thunder. A last cry, "It is accomplished!" Silence.

"I wonder," said man, looking back at the slumped and stricken form. "Was all that really necessary? After all, it was only a little sin . . . He had such a way with people, too."

CHAPTER 14

No One Understands

Tears stained my pillow as I grieved for my handicapped child. The night accentuated the loneliness I felt, and in my sorrow I cried out to Heaven at the injustice she suffered. "Please, God! How my heart aches for her! She's innocent and deserves so much better. It's just not fair! Why must she suffer so?"

It was then that the angel came. "I've been sent to tell you about another Child who was born with a handicap," I was told. "For this Child, it was a terminal one.

"The child lived only 33 years and during those years nearly died a dozen times. His parents were separated before His birth, and throughout the years His Father—from a distance—watched Him grow, knowing that things would get much worse before ever they got better.

"Right from the start it seemed that this Child was to have an uphill battle. He was born more or less outdoors on a cold night, with conditions that could hardly be considered sanitary. When He was only a few days old, His mother had to flee with Him to a foreign country to escape the plottings of a demonic king who wished the Infant dead.

"As this Baby became a boy, His parents' hearts ached for reasons other than concern about His physical safety. Because of His handicap, this Boy didn't do a lot of things that other children did, and He was often left out or laughed at. He had to attend a special school, and the kids He'd see in the neighborhood or at church would sometimes say hurtful things because of that.

"He was a good boy, and His parents loved Him dearly, but He had to be carefully kept, and this was of particular concern to His mother, who often seemed to have to provide most of the specialized care alone.

"Once when He was still a boy, His mother thought that she had lost Him for good, but after three anxious days it looked like He would be all right, and she breathed easier. It should be said, however, that even during those times when His life assumed a degree of normalcy His mother's heart felt the steady prick of a sword, for His future was uncertain.

"As the Boy grew older He came to understand that for reasons pertaining to His handicap, He would never be able to marry or have a family of His own. This was especially hard for Him because He was, above all else, a lover.

"For a time He worked with His hands, but eventually He took up a completely different line of work, and His mother watched Him with mixed emotions. At first it appeared that He was going to make quite a mark in the world, but in less than three years she came to realize that His work would be cut short.

"He had heart trouble, you see, and it finally got the best of Him. His life had always been an uphill battle, but when He climbed that last hill, it proved too much for Him.

"His parents were not together when He died, but they were both on hand to see it happen. One of the Young Man's friends tried to be of some support to His mother, but no one was there to wipe His Father's tears. The Father had been away for most of the Child's life. It had been indescribably difficult for Him, and He tried to come to His Son at the end, but the Young Man was in such bad shape that He was unaware of His Father's presence.

"When His Son died, they say the Father's cries could be heard around the world. Perhaps that's just a figure of speech, but perhaps for those who have ears to hear, it's a reality."

The angel put a hand upon my shoulder. "Child," he said, "if misery loves company, you have some of the best. I care, but *He* understands."

CHAPTER 15

Have You Ever?

D
o you know what it's like to be lonely? So alone that your own thoughts are your only companions? Do you know what it's like as a child to want to play with other children and meet only ridicule?

Do you know what it's like to wish for a retreat in the quiet of your own home, but even there find laughter and sarcasm? Do you know what it's like to spend hours, days, and nights in the lonely refuge of mountain or desert? Do you know what it's like to sit high on a lonely mountain overlooking a city, wishing you could be someone's friend? Do you know how it feels to sleep on rough ground without a blanket year after year?

Have you ever walked through a crowd, attended a dinner party, or passed through a marketplace teeming with people yet somehow still felt alone? Have you ever watched from the shadows while others enjoyed an activity or game? Have you ever been invited by someone to get acquainted and then been asked to come after dark so no one would glimpse you together?

Have you ever fed a large crowd and discovered that the food you provided was more appreciated than you were?

Have you ever walked for days along a hot, dusty highway and finally reached a town, only to be asked to leave?

Have you ever walked 30 miles to comfort a bereaved family, only to be treated as if it were *your* fault that the sick person had died? Have you ever been turned away no matter where you went or whom you asked for lodging?

Have you ever returned to your hometown acquaintances, seeking to give friendship, and had rocks thrown at you? Do you know how it hurts to have no one to talk to, no one to share with, even if that person would only listen?

Have you ever cried so hard that your eyes ached and, trying to talk, you could only moan between sobs? Have you ever spent nights in tears that no one will ever know of except you?

Have you ever thought you had found a few who accepted you as their friend and then watched as they left or ignored you so as not to be embarrassed by you? Have you ever felt the pain of rejection or the bitter disappointment of broken trust? Have you ever given of yourself until there was nothing left to give and then heard mocking laughter because you were so vulnerable?

Have you ever sat alone by the edge of a lake and watched gulls drift above the water, wishing you could fly away? Have you ever struggled against giving up the effort to give of yourself, struggled until you actually sweat blood?

Have you ever spent entire nights worrying and praying for a troubled friend? Have you gone to that same friend for comfort and understanding and heard him say, "I'm too tired to listen"?

Have you ever had people follow you everywhere so that they might distort something you say and justify putting you to death? Have you ever been rudely jostled by calloused men, helpless within their menacing circle, because of love? Have you ever had someone spit upon your bruised and bleeding face? Have you ever felt blood trickle down your back from torn flesh while being beaten by a leather whip with metal strips attached to it?

Have you ever felt the sharp pain of thorns forcefully pressed deep into your scalp and temples? Have you ever had to wipe your eyes with a blood-sopped sleeve in order to see through tears? Do you know how it feels to struggle through your own blood while dragging heavy timbers? Do you think you could stagger on, willingly, toward dying for those who hate, despise, and reject you? Would you bear screaming insults, laughter, and mockery as you collapsed beneath your instrument of death? Would you struggle desperately to rise and continue toward your place of execution?

Have you ever felt the tearing, grinding crunch of nails being pounded through your hands and feet? Have you ever felt, with every nerve, the jolting thud of a cross dropped into its deeply dug hole? Have you ever hung from nails, with open wounds gaping ever wider while crowds taunted, throwing rocks at your bruised and lacerated body? Have you ever hung outstretched as rain and wind buffeted your exhausted body against a cross?

Have you ever gasped hoarsely for breath, aware that you are dying? Do you know how it feels to have vision grow dim as your eyes glaze? Have you ever exhaled your last breath, knowing it is finished?

Have you ever hurt? Have you ever ached? Have you ever suffered? Have you ever died—alone—for people who refused to let you be their friend?

While on this earth, Jesus longed for companionship. He still does. Will you be His friend?

CHAPTER 16

He Is
the Good News

Plenty of bad news is floating around! In fact, Thoreau had it right when he said, "I suppose the news for the next hundred years might be fairly accurately written today." For the most part, as long as people have reported news, it has been depressingly the same. Stories of murder, violence, catastrophe, war, famine, pestilence, promiscuity, abuse, theft, and financial ruin scream at us from the radio, television, and newspapers.

But there is *good news!* It was first given in Eden when the sorrowful pair were promised that a Deliverer would crush the serpent's head. It was later published in the Good News Letter (called by some the Holy Bible) and even proclaimed by angels over Bethlehem's moonlit plain. The good news is really a Person!

Are you troubled or confused? He is called "Wonderful Counsellor" (Isa. 9:6). Are you filled with tension? He is the "Prince of Peace" (verse 6). Is your life full of uncertainties? He is the "Cornerstone" (Ps. 118:22). He is the solid "Rock" on which you can depend (1 Cor. 10:4). Have loved ones or friends let you down? He is "faithful" (Rev. 1:5). Are you lonely? He is the "friend that sticketh closer than a brother" (Prov. 18:24). Do you feel as if there is no one on your side? He is your "advocate" (1 John 2:1). Have you lost your way? He is the "true Light, which lighteth every man that cometh into the world" (John

1:9). Have you gotten yourself into a jam that looks hopeless? He is the "Deliverer" (Rom. 11:26). Is your heart wicked and full of sin? He is your "Righteousness" (Jer. 23:6). Do you feel helpless? He is called "Saviour" (Luke 2:11). Have you lost a loved one in death? He is the "Resurrection, and the Life" (John 11:25). Are you hungry or thirsty for something more in your life? He is the "true bread from heaven" (John 6:32). Are you searching for eternal life? He is the "way, the truth, and the life" (John 14:6). He is Jesus Christ, King of kings, Lord of lords, and He is *your* friend as well!

Tell Me Again

(Based on John 21:25)

HE LIVED WITH US, IMMANUEL.
FOR CENTURIES NOW WE'VE TRIED TO TELL
ABOUT HIS LIFE ON EARTH WITH MEN
AND HOW HE CAME TO COME AGAIN.

WE'VE TOLD THE STORIES O'ER AND O'ER,
AND STILL WE TRY TO TELL THEM MORE
BECAUSE SOMEHOW THEY DON'T GROW OLD—
THESE GREATEST STORIES EVER TOLD.

IF ALL HE DID WERE WRITTEN DOWN,
A BOOK TO HOLD WOULD SCARCE BE FOUND,
FOR ALL THE WORLD COULD NOT CONTAIN
THE STORIES TOLD ABOUT THE NAME.

STILL, WE WILL WRITE AND SPEAK AND SING
ABOUT THE LAMB—OUR COMING KING.
AND SOMEDAY NEAR A SEA OF FIRE
WITH ANGELS WE WILL SING STILL HIGHER.

"WORTHY, WORTHY," WE WILL SAY,
"IS HE WHO STOOPED TO COME OUR WAY."
AND AT HIS FEET WILL BE CAST DOWN,
BY THOSE REDEEMED, UNNUMBERED CROWNS.